Basic Legal Research Workbook

Revised Fourth Edition

EDITORIAL ADVISORS

Erwin Chemerinsky
Dean and Distinguished Professor of Law
Raymond Pryke Professor of First Amendment Law
University of California, Irvine School of Law

Richard A. Epstein
Laurence A. Tisch Professor of Law
New York University School of Law
Peter and Kirsten Bedford Senior Fellow
The Hoover Institution
Senior Lecturer in Law
The University of Chicago

Ronald J. Gilson
Charles J. Meyers Professor of Law and Business
Stanford University
Marc and Eva Stern Professor of Law and Business
Columbia Law School

James E. Krier
Earl Warren DeLano Professor of Law
The University of Michigan Law School

Richard K. Neumann, Jr.
Professor of Law
Maurice A. Deane School of Law at Hofstra University

Robert H. Sitkoff
John L. Gray Professor of Law
Harvard Law School

David Alan Sklansky
Professor of Law
Stanford Law School

ASPEN COURSEBOOK SERIES

Basic Legal Research Workbook

Revised Fourth Edition

Amy E. Sloan
Associate Dean for Academic Affairs and Professor of Law
University of Baltimore School of Law

Steven D. Schwinn
Associate Professor of Law
The John Marshall Law School

John D. Edwards
Professor of Law
Drake University Law School

Wolters Kluwer

Copyright © 2015 Amy E. Sloan and Steven D. Schwinn.

Published by Wolters Kluwer in New York.

Wolters Kluwer serves customers worldwide with CCH, Aspen Publishers, and Kluwer Law International products. (www.wolterskluwerlb.com)

No part of this publication may be reproduced or transmitted in any form or by any means, electronic or mechanical, including photocopy, recording, or utilized by any information storage or retrieval system, without written permission from the publisher. For information about permissions or to request permissions online, visit us at www.wolterskluwerlb.com, or a written request may be faxed to our permissions department at 212-771-0803.

To contact Customer Service, e-mail customer.service@wolterskluwer.com,
call 1-800-234-1660, fax 1-800-901-9075, or mail correspondence to:

> Wolters Kluwer
> Attn: Order Department
> PO Box 990
> Frederick, MD 21705

Printed in the United States of America.

1 2 3 4 5 6 7 8 9 0

ISBN 978-1-4548-5041-0

About Wolters Kluwer Law & Business

Wolters Kluwer Law & Business is a leading global provider of intelligent information and digital solutions for legal and business professionals in key specialty areas, and respected educational resources for professors and law students. Wolters Kluwer Law & Business connects legal and business professionals as well as those in the education market with timely, specialized authoritative content and information-enabled solutions to support success through productivity, accuracy and mobility.

Serving customers worldwide, Wolters Kluwer Law & Business products include those under the Aspen Publishers, CCH, Kluwer Law International, Loislaw, ftwilliam.com and MediRegs family of products.

CCH products have been a trusted resource since 1913, and are highly regarded resources for legal, securities, antitrust and trade regulation, government contracting, banking, pension, payroll, employment and labor, and healthcare reimbursement and compliance professionals.

Aspen Publishers products provide essential information to attorneys, business professionals and law students. Written by preeminent authorities, the product line offers analytical and practical information in a range of specialty practice areas from securities law and intellectual property to mergers and acquisitions and pension/benefits. Aspen's trusted legal education resources provide professors and students with high-quality, up-to-date and effective resources for successful instruction and study in all areas of the law.

Kluwer Law International products provide the global business community with reliable international legal information in English. Legal practitioners, corporate counsel and business executives around the world rely on Kluwer Law journals, looseleafs, books, and electronic products for comprehensive information in many areas of international legal practice.

Loislaw is a comprehensive online legal research product providing legal content to law firm practitioners of various specializations. Loislaw provides attorneys with the ability to quickly and efficiently find the necessary legal information they need, when and where they need it, by facilitating access to primary law as well as state-specific law, records, forms and treatises.

ftwilliam.com offers employee benefits professionals the highest quality plan documents (retirement, welfare and non-qualified) and government forms (5500/PBGC, 1099 and IRS) software at highly competitive prices.

MediRegs products provide integrated health care compliance content and software solutions for professionals in healthcare, higher education and life sciences, including professionals in accounting, law and consulting.

Wolters Kluwer Law & Business, a division of Wolters Kluwer, is headquartered in New York. Wolters Kluwer is a market-leading global information services company focused on professionals.

*This book is dedicated in memory of the Honorable Philip Townsend Cole,
who always emphasized the importance of accurate research.*

Contents

Preface   *xi*
Acknowledgments   *xv*
General Instructions   *xvii*

Chapter 1: Introduction to Legal Research   1

| Exercise 1.1 | Introduction to Print Research | 1 |
| Exercise 1.2 | Introduction to Electronic Research | 13 |

Chapter 2: Generating Search Terms   19

| Exercise 2.1 | Generating Search Terms | 19 |
| Exercise 2.1 | Charts 1-8 | 21 |

Chapter 3: Secondary Source Research   29

Exercise 3.1	Researching Legal Encyclopedias and A.L.R. Annotations in Print	29
Exercise 3.2	Researching Secondary Sources Electronically	41
Exercise 3.3	Researching Secondary Sources on Your Own	49

Chapter 4: Case Research   53

Exercise 4.1	Researching Cases in Print	53
Exercise 4.2	Researching Cases Electronically	61
Exercise 4.3	Researching Cases on Your Own	69

Chapter 5: Research with Citators   73

Exercise 5.1	Researching Cases with Citators	73
Exercise 5.2	Researching Statutes and Secondary Sources with Citators	81
Exercise 5.3	Checking Case Citations on Your Own	85

Chapter 6: Statutory Research   89

Exercise 6.1	Researching Statutes in Print	89
Exercise 6.2	Researching Statutes Electronically	97
Exercise 6.3	Researching Statutes on Your Own	107

Chapter 7: Federal Legislative History Research   111

| Exercise 7.1 | Researching the Legislative History of a Federal Statute Using Statutory Annotations | 111 |

Exercise 7.2	Researching the Legislative History of a Federal Statute by Subject	117
Exercise 7.3	Researching the Legislative History of a Federal Statute with Congress.gov	123

Chapter 8: Federal Administrative Law Research — 127

Exercise 8.1	Researching Federal Administrative Regulations from a Statute	127
Exercise 8.2	Researching Federal Administrative Regulations Using Government Web Sites	133
Exercise 8.3	Researching Federal Administrative Regulations on Your Own	137

Chapter 9: Electronic Search Techniques — 139

Exercise 9.1	Electronic Search Techniques	139

Chapter 10: Research Planning — 149

Exercise 10.1	Developing and Executing a Research Plan	149

Preface

The revised fourth edition of *Basic Legal Research Workbook* contains updated instructions for electronic research exercises that reflect the changes in Westlaw and Lexis. In particular, the updated instructions are keyed only to WestlawNext and Lexis Advance (and not to the now-defunct Westlaw Classic and earlier Lexis.com platforms). The revised fourth edition also contains minor updates to certain other electronic research platforms and book exercises to reflect changes in those resources. Otherwise, the revised fourth edition contains all the exercises, features, and coverage of the fourth edition, including the following:

- Updated problem sets—The text contains updated versions of the fourth edition's problem sets.
- Electronic research—New questions highlighting features specific to WestlawNext and Lexis Advance are included, as is coverage of Google Scholar.
- Print research—Throughout the text, coverage of print research has been revised to accommodate changes in library holdings. Chapter 4 (Case Research) and Chapter 6 (Statutory Research) include options for you to assign additional jurisdictions not specified in the exercises. This allows you to customize the assignments to fit with your library's holdings. In Chapter 7 (Federal Legislative History Research) and Chapter 8 (Federal Administrative Law Research), students have the option of using a mix of print and electronic sources or using electronic sources exclusively to complete the exercises.

The revised fourth edition also includes a new collaborator, John Edwards. Professor Edwards is a long-time user of the Workbook and has provided invaluable feedback over the years. We are very excited to include Professor Edwards on the revised fourth edition.

The philosophy and organization of the revised fourth edition remain the same as those of the prior editions. *Basic Legal Research Workbook* contains library exercises that allow students to learn about the scope and organization of research sources, that guide them through the research process, and that reinforce their skills through assignments requiring independent work.

The Workbook is designed to help students learn both the mechanics and the process of legal research through a combination of guided and unguided research assignments. In the guided assignments, the questions gradually increase in complexity. Review questions test students' understanding of the nature and organization of the sources they are using. Research questions early in an assignment direct students through the research process. Later questions ask for information, but require students to research more independently. The unguided research assignments require open research. Students generate their own search terms and follow their own research paths to locate legal authority.

Each assignment, whether guided or unguided, incorporates hypothetical fact patterns and legal questions that students must answer based on the results of their research. Thus, students must not only go through the steps of using each resource in an assignment, they must also read and apply what they find.

The Workbook's coverage is comprehensive. It contains exercises covering a wide range of legal research resources in both print and electronic format. Chapter 1 contains introductory assignments designed to acquaint students with the organization of the law library and basic features of print and electronic research sources. Chapter 2 contains information on generating search terms, as well as a series of charts that students can use to generate search terms for later assignments in this Workbook or any open research project.

Chapters 3 through 8 each contain three exercises. Chapter 3, Secondary Source Research, covers research with legal encyclopedias, A.L.R. Annotations, legal periodicals, and treatises. Chapter 4, Case Research, addresses research with print digests and electronic sources. In Chapter 5, Research with Citators, students learn about electronic citators for cases and other forms of authority. Chapter 6, Statutory Research, covers state and federal research in both print and electronic sources. Chapter 7, Federal Legislative History Research, and Chapter 8, Federal Administrative Law Research, provide instruction in the most commonly used sources of federal law on these topics.

Chapter 9, Electronic Search Techniques, illustrates a variety of strategies for effective Boolean searching, including appropriate use of connectors and use of functions such as Field searches. It also demonstrates how to use Boolean searches in WestlawNext and Lexis Advance. Although it is the penultimate chapter, it can be assigned as soon as students have completed basic instruction in electronic research. Chapter 10 covers Research Planning. It contains hypothetical fact patterns that require students to develop and execute a research strategy using multiple sources of authority.

Each assignment follows a consistent organization that students should find easy to follow. In addition to containing research questions, each assignment also contains some textual material on the resource it covers. This is to provide context for the material and explain what students are likely to see in the books or online. The research questions in each assignment are fairly generic. Students use additional information in charts containing problem sets to answer the questions. Professors can assign problem sets or allow students to choose their own.

The organization of each chapter gives professors the flexibility to assign exercises that fit with the structure and pace of their courses. Every exercise in every chapter is a free-standing assignment. Therefore, professors can assign the exercises in any order. Professors who integrate instruction in print and electronic research can assign exercises on both for each research source covered in the Workbook. Alternatively, those who cover print research before electronic research can assign the print research assignments first, saving the electronic research assignments for later in the course. The unguided research assignments work with either print or electronic research tools and can be assigned with the guided research exercises or separately as a review of the research process.

The number of problem sets for each assignment adds to the Workbook's flexibility. Each chapter contains multiple problem sets for print research to distribute students throughout the library. Most print exercises have 15 print problem sets lettered A to O. Therefore, professors can assign each exercise to a large number of students who will be working in the same law library without creating competition for resources. For professors who coordinate instruction in research and writing, the problem sets cover a wide range of topics that can lend themselves to a number of potential writing projects.

Although *Basic Legal Research Workbook* contains some textual material interspersed with the research questions, it is not a self-instructional workbook. Students will need to read a research text, receive classroom instruction, or both to complete the assignments successfully and become adept at legal research. The Workbook is tailored to complement *Basic Legal Research: Tools and Strategies*. It can, however, be used with other research texts as well. In addition, the Workbook does not provide citation instruction. It covers research process, not citation format.

Both teaching and learning legal research are challenging undertakings. We hope that students using this Workbook will find it to be an engaging resource for learning the fundamentals of legal research. We hope professors will find it similarly engaging, as well as adaptable to a variety of course structures and teaching techniques.

Amy E. Sloan
Steven D. Schwinn
John D. Edwards
June 2015

Acknowledgments

Many people assisted us in writing the revised fourth edition of this text, and we would like to acknowledge their contributions. Our students, of course, continue to be a source of inspiration. We would also like to thank the people at Wolters Kluwer Legal Education who helped make this project a reality: Carol McGeehan, Barbara Roth, Elizabeth Kenny, and their colleagues, as well as Troy Froebe, Kathy Langone, Andrew Blevins, and their colleagues at The Froebe Group. We also received invaluable feedback from anonymous reviewers and would like to thank them for taking the time to share their thoughts and suggestions.

Amy Sloan would also like to thank a number of people who assisted with this book. The staff members at the University of Baltimore Law Library were, as always, a great help. Special thanks go to Catherine Simanski for providing research assistance. I would also like to thank Peggy, Drew, and Jack for the support and inspiration they provided.

Steven Schwinn would like to thank the faculty and staff at the John Marshall Law School Law Library. Special thanks go to Greta Berna for her research assistance. I would also like to thank Susie, Caroline, and Andrew for their support.

John Edwards would like to thank the faculty and staff of the Drake University Law Library. I would also like to express my appreciation to our Legal Research and Writing teaching assistants who tested assignments and made suggestions for improvement. Special thanks go to Robert Evans for his lead role in that process. Having the support of Beth Ann, Craig, Martha, Chris, and Brooks helped make the project a success.

General Instructions

These general instructions explain the structure of the exercises in this Workbook and will help you get the most out of each assignment. You should read them before you start the first assignment and refer back to them as necessary for later assignments. Occasionally, the underlying research sources change so significantly that it is necessary to update the exercises. This is especially true for exercises covering Westlaw and Lexis. Both of these vendors have recently introduced new versions of their research products and may continue to revise the look and coverage of information in the new versions. You can check for updates at www.aspenlawschool.com/sloan_workbook.

I. Using the Problem Set Charts

Many of the exercises contain multiple problem sets so that everyone in your class can work on the same assignment without needing to use the same materials at the same time. The research questions in the exercises are generic questions for all the problem sets. You will need to use additional information provided for your problem set to answer the questions.

The additional information for the problem sets appears in the problem set charts interspersed with the questions. Problem sets are identified by letter (A, B, C, etc.). If your professor does not assign a problem set for you to use, you can use any problem set to complete the assignment.

II. Working on the Exercises

A. Read the Goals and Instructions

Each exercise begins with information about the assignment that you should read before you get started. The goals of the assignment and the specific instructions you should follow are set out at the beginning. The exercises will make the most sense to you if you know what you should get out of them and how to approach them. After the general instructions, you will find a section entitled "The Assignment." This section provides an overview of the assignment and should be reviewed before you begin your work.

B. Answer the Questions

As you work on the questions, keep in mind that the answers should be fairly straightforward. If you find information that seems to answer a question, it probably answers the question. You should not expect the answers to jump off the page or computer screen, and you certainly need to read the questions carefully and follow all the research steps to answer them. The questions do not, however, contain hidden tricks or traps, and you should not read more into the questions than is there. The simplest answer will usually be the correct one.

Many of the questions contain hints to help you locate information to complete the exercise. The hints are intended to address aspects of the assignment that may raise questions. Be sure to read the hints carefully and follow them whenever they are provided.

Many of the questions require you to explain your answer. A simple yes or no will not suffice when the question asks for an explanation. Unless your professor requests something different, you should state your conclusion, summarize the legal rule on which you rely, and show how the facts of the hypothetical apply to the law. In most instances, you will be able to do this with a sentence or two of explanation.

For example, assume you were working on a research question asking whether a contract to sell illegal drugs is enforceable in court if it is breached, and assume you found a case saying that drug dealing contracts are not enforceable because they involve illegal activity. It would not be sufficient for you simply to answer "no" to the question. Instead, your answer should look something like this:

> No. Courts will not enforce contracts to perform illegal activities. The drug dealing contract in this case involves illegal activity. Therefore, the courts will not enforce it.

C. Ask for Help if You Get Sidetracked

Each exercise contains a time limit. Most of the time limits set the maximum amount of time you should spend working on individual questions. Some set the maximum amount of time you should spend on the entire exercise. **Follow these limits.** If you are taking longer than the time allotted to complete your work, you should stop and ask for help from your professor, a reference librarian, or another authorized person, such as a teaching assistant. Do not ask your classmates for help unless you are permitted to collaborate on research.

There are several common ways to get sidetracked on a research assignment. Following the troubleshooting hints below will help keep you from getting stuck in your research.

Here are some troubleshooting hints for print research:

- **Are you looking in the correct block in the problem set chart?** If not, you may be looking for something that does not exist in the jurisdiction or resource for your problem set.
- **Are you following any hints provided with the questions?** Be sure to read the hints carefully and follow them whenever they are provided.
- **Is the book you need off the shelf?** Someone else may be using the book, or it may be mis-shelved. A reference librarian can help you locate a missing book.
- **Are you looking in the correct book?** Be sure to check the volume number, if applicable. You should also check that you are using the correct edition or series in a set with multiple editions or series.
- **Are you looking in the correct place in the book?** Be sure to check the page number, if applicable. You should also check that you are looking in the right section if the book contains multiple types of information. If a research question directs you to use specific search terms in an index, be sure to use the search terms provided.

- **Have you remembered to follow every step in the research process for the resource you are using?** The most common reminder students need in conducting print research is, "Did you check the pocket part?"

Here are some troubleshooting hints for electronic research:

- **Are you looking in the correct block in the problem set chart?** If not, you may be looking for something that does not exist in the jurisdiction or resource for your problem set.
- **Are you following any hints provided with the questions?** Be sure to read the hints carefully and follow them whenever they are provided.
- **Are you using the correct service and following the instructions for using that service?** If a question specifically directs you to use a particular research service, the instructions will not work for a different service.
- **Are you using the correct database, function, or command?** Although there is usually more than one way to locate an authority in an electronic service, the research questions are tailored to the databases, functions, and commands specified in the questions.
- **Have you typed the search information correctly?** Typographical and punctuation errors will affect the search results. If a research question directs you to use a specific search, be sure to enter it exactly as it appears in the exercise.

Although following these hints will get you back on track in most situations, they may not always work. You should keep in mind that legal research is dynamic, but the exercises are static. Once they are printed, they cannot change to account for changes in the books, the computer interface, or the law. Therefore, if what you find does not seem to fit with the research questions, you should get help. You should also check online for any updates. If updates are available, you can find them at www.aspenlawschool.com/sloan_workbook.

Of course, starting an exercise well before it is due is another way to avoid difficulties. Although the exercises are structured to distribute students throughout the library, there are still likely to be at least some other students using the same resources you need to use. As the due date for an exercise approaches, books are more likely to be in use or mis-shelved, which will make completing the assignment more difficult for you. Most people, and especially lawyers, respond to deadline pressure and organize their work accordingly. If you can motivate yourself to do the work early, it will make these exercises easier for you.

Chapter 1
INTRODUCTION TO LEGAL RESEARCH

Exercise 1.1
Introduction to Print Research

Name: _____   Due Date: _____

Professor: _____   Section: _____

Goals

1. To learn the different types of authority and how to distinguish among them.
2. To locate constitutional provisions, statutes, and cases from their citations.
3. To become familiar with the format of constitutional provisions, statutes, and cases.

Instructions

1. After each question, you will find space to write your answer. This is for your convenience while you are working on the exercise. After you finish your research, submit your answers in typewritten form on a separate answer sheet. Do not retype the questions. Your answer sheet should contain only the answers to the questions.

2. If you spend more than 15 minutes trying to find the answer to any individual question, use the troubleshooting hints in the General Instructions for this Workbook. If you are still unable to find the answer, stop and seek assistance.

3. Reshelve all books as soon as you finish using them.

Problem Set

(circle one)   A   B   C   D   E   F   G   H   I   J   K   L   M   N   O

THE ASSIGNMENT

This exercise will acquaint you with the locations and formats of federal and state legal authorities. You will locate federal and state constitutions, statutes, and cases, and answer some questions about what you find.

I. Review Questions

   A. Explain the difference between primary and secondary authorities, and give an example of each.

   B. Explain the difference between mandatory and persuasive authorities, and give an example of each.

   C. When is secondary authority useful? Is it ever binding? Why or why not?

II. Locating Constitutional Provisions in Print

   ### A. United States Constitution

The United States Constitution is the preeminent law of the land. All other laws, both federal and state, must comport with the federal Constitution. Because of its preeminence in the legal system, the federal Constitution is often published along with statutes passed by legislatures in sets of books called "codes."

When Congress passes federal legislation which is signed into law by the President, the resulting statutes are published in the federal code, which is discussed in more detail below. The federal Constitution is published with the federal code. State statutes are also published in codes. Every state has its own code. The federal Constitution is published in most (but not all) state codes.

For the questions below, you need to locate the code specified for your problem set in the following charts. Then you need to locate the federal Constitution within the code and look up two constitutional provisions specified in the questions following the charts. When you locate the appropriate provisions, you may see a series of notes following them, including summaries of cases interpreting the provisions. These notes are called "annotations." They are research tools you will learn to use later in your legal research class. You do not need to read the annotations to answer the questions in this exercise.

You may also find a soft cover booklet called a "pocket part" inserted into the back cover of the book. Pocket parts are used to update information in the hardcover volume. You will learn to use pocket parts later in your legal research class. You do not need to refer to the pocket part for this exercise.

Locate the code for your problem set, and locate the United States Constitution within the code to answer the questions below. (Hints: Use the labels on the spines of the books to locate the volume or volumes containing the Constitution. Constitutions usually appear in separate volumes near the beginning or the end of the set. If you use a state code, be sure to locate the United States Constitution, not the state constitution, to answer the questions.)

State and Code—United States Constitution

Problem Set A	Arkansas	*Arkansas Code of 1987 Annotated*
Problem Set B	Indiana	*Burns Indiana Statutes Annotated*
Problem Set C	Mississippi	*Mississippi Code 1972 Annotated* or *West's Annotated Mississippi Code*
Problem Set D	New Mexico	*New Mexico Statutes 1978 Annotated*
Problem Set E	Michigan	*Michigan Compiled Laws Annotated*
Problem Set F	Connecticut	*Connecticut General Statutes Annotated*
Problem Set G	Georgia	*Official Code of Georgia Annotated*
Problem Set H	Florida	*West's Florida Statutes Annotated*
Problem Set I	Colorado	*Colorado Revised Statutes Annotated*
Problem Set J	Ohio	*Baldwin's* or *Page's Ohio Revised Code Annotated*
Problem Set K	Alabama	*Michie's Alabama Code of 1975* (Hint: Some volumes may be labeled *Code of Alabama of 1975*.)
Problem Set L	North Carolina	*General Statutes of North Carolina Annotated*
Problem Set M	Iowa	*Iowa Code Annotated*
Problem Set N	Kentucky	*Baldwin's Kentucky Revised Statutes Annotated* or *Michie's Kentucky Revised Statutes Annotated*
Problem Set O	Minnesota	*Minnesota Statutes Annotated*

1. Locate Article III, § 1, in the United States Constitution. Briefly describe what this section provides.

2. Locate Amendment I in the United States Constitution. Briefly describe what this amendment provides. (Hint for Problem Sets J and M: The state code labels the amendments to the federal Constitution as "Articles." Look for the section that refers to articles in addition to, and amendments of, the Constitution.)

3. Are these provisions primary or secondary authority?

4. Are these provisions mandatory or persuasive authority for the state courts in the state for your problem set?

B. State Constitutions

As noted above, all laws, both state and federal, must comport with the federal Constitution. Each state also has its own constitution. The constitution is created by a state constitutional convention, and it defines the authority granted to the state's government. All state laws must comport with that state's constitution. One place to find a state's constitution is in the state code.

When you locate a state constitutional provision, you may find annotations with research notes following the text of the provision. You will learn to use the annotations later in your legal research class. You do not need to read the annotations to answer the questions in this exercise.

You may also find a pocket part update inserted into the back cover of the book. You will learn to use pocket parts later in your legal research class. You do not need to refer to the pocket part for this exercise.

Use the state code to locate the constitution for the state for your problem set. Locate the provisions indicated for your problem set, and answer the questions below. (Hint: Many state codes include old versions of the state constitution. Be sure to use the most recent version of the state constitution.)

1. Briefly describe what the first provision for your problem set provides.

First Provision—State Constitution

Problem Set A	Article 4, § 1
Problem Set B	Article 7, § 1
Problem Set C	Article 6, § 144
Problem Set D	Article VI, § 1
Problem Set E	Article VI, § 1
Problem Set F	Article 5, § 1
Problem Set G	Article VI, § 1, Paragraph 1
Problem Set H	Article 5, § 1
Problem Set I	Article 6, § 1
Problem Set J	Article IV, § 1
Problem Set K	Article VI, § 139
Problem Set L	Article IV, § 1
Problem Set M	Article 5, § 1
Problem Set N	§ 109
Problem Set O	Article 6, § 1

2. Briefly describe what the second provision for your problem set provides.

Second Provision—State Constitution

Problem Set A	Article 2, § 6
Problem Set B	Article 1, § 9
Problem Set C	Article 3, § 13
Problem Set D	Article II, § 17
Problem Set E	Article I, § 5
Problem Set F	Article 1, § 4
Problem Set G	Article I, § 1, Paragraph 5
Problem Set H	Article 1, § 4
Problem Set I	Article 2, § 10

6 Basic Legal Research Workbook

Problem Set J	Article I, § 11
Problem Set K	Article I, § 4
Problem Set L	Article I, § 14
Problem Set M	Article 1, § 7
Problem Set N	§ 8
Problem Set O	Article 1, § 3

3. Are these provisions of the state constitution primary or secondary authority?

4. Are these provisions of the state constitution mandatory or persuasive authority for the state courts in that state?

III. Locating State Statutes and Cases in Print

A. State Statutes

As noted above, when a state legislature passes legislation (pursuant to power granted to it by the state constitution), the resulting statutes are published in the state code.

When you locate a provision of a state code, sometimes you will find a series of notes following the provision, including summaries of cases interpreting the provision. These notes are called "annotations." They are research tools you will learn to use later in your legal research class. You do not need to read the annotations to answer the questions in this exercise.

You may also find a pocket part update inserted into the back cover of the book. You will learn to use pocket parts later in your legal research class. You do not need to refer to the pocket part for this exercise.

To see the format of a state statute, locate the state statute for your problem set, and answer the questions below.

State Statute

Problem Set A	*Arkansas Code of 1987 Annotated* § 5-39-201
Problem Set B	*Burns Indiana Statutes Annotated* § 35-43-2-1
Problem Set C	*Mississippi Code 1972 Annotated* or *West's Annotated Mississippi Code* § 97-17-23

Problem Set D	*New Mexico Statutes 1978 Annotated* § 30-16-3
Problem Set E	*Michigan Compiled Laws Annotated* § 750.110
Problem Set F	*Connecticut General Statutes Annotated* § 42a-2-302
Problem Set G	*Official Code of Georgia Annotated* § 11-2-302
Problem Set H	*West's Florida Statutes Annotated* § 672.302
Problem Set I	*Colorado Revised Statutes Annotated* § 4-2-302
Problem Set J	*Baldwin's* or *Page's Ohio Revised Code Annotated* § 1302.15
Problem Set K	*Code of Alabama of 1975* § 6-11-20
Problem Set L	*General Statutes of North Carolina Annotated* § 1D-15
Problem Set M	*Iowa Code Annotated* § 668A.1
Problem Set N	*Baldwin's* or *Michie's Kentucky Revised Statutes Annotated* § 411.186
Problem Set O	*Minnesota Statutes Annotated* § 549.20

1. Provide the name of the section. You will find this next to the section number.

2. Briefly describe what this section provides.

B. State Cases

When courts decide cases, the opinions are published in books called "reporters." Some states publish reporters containing only cases decided by the courts of that state. There are also sets of reporters called "regional reporters" that compile cases from several states within a particular geographic region. To answer the following questions, you will need to find the regional reporters.

Locate the state case for your problem set, and answer the questions below. (Hint: The regional reporters have multiple series (2d, 3d). When you locate the reporter, be sure you are looking in the correct series.)

State Case

Problem Set A	*Winters v. State*, volume 848, *South Western Reporter*, 2d series, page 441
Problem Set B	*Gebhart v. State*, volume 525, *North Eastern Reporter*, 2d series, page 603

Problem Set C	*Wheeler v. State*, volume 826, *Southern Reporter*, 2d series, page 731
Problem Set D	*State v. Gregory*, volume 869, *Pacific Reporter*, 2d series, page 292
Problem Set E	*People v. Toole*, volume 576, *North Western Reporter*, 2d series, page 441
Problem Set F	*Iamartino v. Avallone*, volume 477, *Atlantic Reporter*, 2d series, page 124
Problem Set G	*Stefan Jewelers, Inc. v. Electro-Protective Corp.*, volume 288, *South Eastern Reporter*, 2d series, page 667
Problem Set H	*Credit Alliance Corp. v. Westland Mach. Co., Inc.*, volume 439, *Southern Reporter*, 2d series, page 332
Problem Set I	*Davis v. M.L.G. Corp.*, volume 712, *Pacific Reporter*, 2d series, page 985
Problem Set J	*Spectrum Networks, Inc. v. Plus Realty, Cincinnati, Inc.*, volume 878, *North Eastern Reporter*, 2d series, page 1122
Problem Set K	*Clark v. Kindley*, volume 10, *Southern Reporter*, 3d series, page 1005
Problem Set L	*Phillips v. Restaurant Management of Carolina, L.P.*, volume 552, *South Eastern Reporter*, 2d series, page 686
Problem Set M	*Kuta v. Newberg*, volume 600, *North Western Reporter*, 2d series, page 280
Problem Set N	*Bierman v. Klapheke*, volume 967, *South Western Reporter*, 2d series, page 16
Problem Set O	*Wikert v. Northern Sand and Gravel, Inc.*, volume 402, *North Western Reporter*, 2d series, page 178

1. Following the name of the case, you will find a reference to the name of the court that decided this case. Provide the name of the court.

2. At the beginning of the case, you will see a synopsis of the decision. After the synopsis, you will see one or more paragraphs summarizing key points within the decision. A summary paragraph begins with a heading in bold type, followed by a key symbol and a number. If more than one summary paragraph appears at the beginning of the case, the paragraphs will be numbered. These summary paragraphs are research references called "headnotes" that you will learn to use later in your legal research class.

    How many headnotes are at the beginning of the case you located?

3. Briefly explain what this case is about, as it relates to the state statute you located. (Hint: Depending on which problem set you complete, the case may be quite long. Limit your explanation to the relationship between the case and the state statutory provision you located. If the case has concurring or dissenting opinions, do not summarize them; limit your explanation to the majority opinion.)

IV. Locating Federal Statutes and Cases in Print

A. Federal Statutes

As noted above, federal statutes are published in the federal code. You can find federal statutes using the *United States Code* (U.S.C.), the *United States Code Annotated* (U.S.C.A.), or the *United States Code Service* (U.S.C.S.).

When you locate a provision of the federal code, you may find annotations with research notes following the text of the provision. You will learn to use the annotations later in your legal research class. You do not need to read the annotations to answer the questions in this exercise.

You may also find a pocket part update inserted into the back cover of the book. You will learn to use pocket parts later in your research class. You do not need to refer to the pocket part for this exercise.

Locate the federal statute for your problem set, and answer the questions below. (Hint: If you use U.S.C. to answer the questions, be sure to use the most current edition.)

Federal Statute—U.S.C., U.S.C.A., or U.S.C.S.

Problem Sets A, B, C, D & E	Title 17, § 102
Problem Sets F, G, H, I & J	Title 29, § 654
Problem Sets K, L, M, N & O	Title 42, § 2000a
	(Hint: Be sure to find § 2000a, not 2000(a) or 2000a-1, 2000a-2, etc.)

1. Provide the name of the section. You will find this next to the section number.

2. Briefly describe what the statute provides.

B. Federal Cases

Like state cases, federal cases are published in reporters. There are different sets of reporters for cases from different levels of the federal courts. For this exercise, you will need to locate one of the following sets of reporters: the *Federal Supplement* or *Federal Supplement, 2d Series*, both of which contain decisions from federal district courts, or the *Federal Reporter, 2d Series*, or *Federal Reporter, 3d Series*, both of which contain cases from the federal courts of appeals.

Locate the federal case for your problem set, and answer the questions below. (Hint: Be sure you are using both the correct reporter and the correct series to locate the federal case.)

Federal Case

Problem Set A	*O'Connor v. Cindy Gerke & Associates, Inc.*, volume 300, *Federal Supplement*, 2d series, page 759
Problem Set B	*Midway Manufacturing Co. v. Strohon*, volume 564, *Federal Supplement*, page 741
Problem Set C	*Hunt v. Pasternack*, volume 179, *Federal Reporter*, 3d series, page 683
Problem Set D	*Torah Soft Ltd. v. Drosnin*, volume 136, *Federal Supplement*, 2d series, page 276
Problem Set E	*Tandy Corp. v. Personal Micro Computers, Inc.*, volume 524, *Federal Supplement*, page 171
Problem Set F	*Safeway, Inc. v. Occupational Safety & Health Review Comm'n*, volume 382, *Federal Reporter*, 3d series, page 1189
Problem Set G	*Anthony Crane Rental, Inc. v. Reich*, volume 70, *Federal Reporter*, 3d series, page 1298
Problem Set H	*Tierdael Construction Co. v. Occupational Safety and Health Review Comm'n*, volume 340, *Federal Reporter*, 3d series, page 1110
Problem Set I	*Brock v. Williams Enterprises of Georgia, Inc.*, volume 832, *Federal Reporter*, 2d series, page 567
Problem Set J	*Brock v. City Oil Well Service Co.*, volume 795, *Federal Reporter*, 2d series, page 507
Problem Set K	*Afkhami v. Carnival Corp.*, volume 305, *Federal Supplement*, 2d series, page 1308
Problem Set L	*Burnette v. Bredesen*, volume 566, *Federal Supplement*, 2d series, page 738
Problem Set M	*Sherman v. Marriott Hotel Services, Inc.*, volume 317, *Federal Supplement*, 2d series, page 609
Problem Set N	*Baker v. Greyhound Bus Line*, volume 240, *Federal Supplement*, 2d series, page 454
Problem Set O	*Rogers v. New York City Board of Elections*, volume 988, *Federal Supplement*, page 409

1. You will find one or more headnotes at the beginning of the case similar to those you saw in the state case. How many headnotes are at the beginning of the case?

2. Following the headnote(s), you will find the name of the judge who wrote the opinion in the case. Provide the judge's name. (Hint: If the case has concurring or dissenting opinions, provide only the name of the judge who wrote the majority opinion.)

3. Briefly explain what this case is about, as it relates to the topic of the federal statutory provisions you located. (Hint: Depending on which problem set you complete, the case may be quite long. Limit your explanation to the relationship between the case and the federal statutory provision you located. If the case has concurring or dissenting opinions, do not summarize them; limit your explanation to the majority opinion.)

Exercise 1.2
Introduction to Electronic Research

Name: _____   Due Date: _____

Professor: _____   Section: _____

Goals

1. To retrieve authorities in Westlaw and Lexis from their citations.
2. To become familiar with the format of authorities in Westlaw and Lexis.
3. To use some of the navigation tools in Westlaw and Lexis to link both to information within the retrieved document and to new documents referenced within the retrieved document.

Instructions

1. After each question, you will find space to write your answer. This is for your convenience while you are working on the exercise. After you finish your research, submit your answers in typewritten form on a separate answer sheet. Do not retype the questions. Your answer sheet should contain only the answers to the questions.

2. If you spend more than 15 minutes trying to find the answer to any individual question, use the troubleshooting hints in the General Instructions for this Workbook. If you are still unable to find the answer, stop and seek assistance.

Problem Set

(circle one)   A   B   C   D   E   F   G   H   I   J   K   L   M   N   O

THE ASSIGNMENT

This exercise requires you to retrieve legal authorities using two of the most commonly used electronic research services, Westlaw and Lexis. Although the text of an authority retrieved using either service will be identical, each service adds its own editorial enhancements and research links to help you locate additional information related to the authority. As a consequence, the format of a document retrieved using one of these services may differ slightly from the format of the same document retrieved in the other.

I. WestlawNext

A. Locating Cases in WestlawNext

Use the global search box in WestlawNext to retrieve a state case from its citation. Retrieve any state case for your problem set **other than** the one you located in print in Exercise 1.1. Do not enter the case name; use only the abbreviated citation provided in the problem set to retrieve the case.

State Case

Problem Sets A, B, C, D & E	(1) *Winters v. State*, 848 S.W.2d 441 (2) *Gebhart v. State*, 525 N.E.2d 603 (3) *Wheeler v. State*, 826 So. 2d 731 (4) *State v. Gregory*, 869 P.2d 292 (5) *People v. Toole*, 576 N.W.2d 441
Problem Sets F, G, H, I & J	(1) *Iamartino v. Avallone*, 477 A.2d 124 (2) *Stefan Jewelers, Inc. v. Electro-Protective Corp.*, 288 S.E.2d 667 (3) *Credit Alliance Corp. v. Westland Mach. Co., Inc.*, 439 So. 2d 332 (4) *Davis v. M.L.G. Corp.*, 712 P.2d 985 (5) *Spectrum Networks, Inc. v. Plus Realty, Cincinnati, Inc.*, 878 N.E.2d 1122
Problem Sets K, L, M, N & O	(1) *Clark v. Kindley*, 10 So. 3d 1005 (2) *Phillips v. Restaurant Management of Carolina, L.P.*, 552 S.E.2d 686 (3) *Kuta v. Newberg*, 600 N.W.2d 280 (4) *Bierman v. Klapheke*, 967 S.W.2d 16 (5) *Wikert v. Northern Sand and Gravel, Inc.*, 402 N.W.2d 178

1. Provide the name of the court that decided the case.

2. How many headnotes appear at the beginning of the case?

3. Read the first headnote in the case. You can use the headnotes to navigate within the case. Click on the 1 in the box with the first headnote in the case.

   Where does this link take you within the document?

B. Locating Statutes in WestlawNext

Use the global search box in WestlawNext to retrieve a state statute from its citation.

Retrieve any state statute for your problem set **other than** the one you located in print in Exercise 1.1. Use the abbreviated citation provided in the problem set to retrieve the statute.

State Statute

Problem Sets A, B, C, D & E	(1) AR ST 5-39-201 (2) IN ST 35-43-2-1 (3) MS ST 97-17-23 (4) NM ST 30-16-3 (5) MI ST 750.110	(Hint: Locate section 35-43-2-1, not 35-43-2-1.5.)
Problem Sets F, G, H, I & J	(1) CT ST 42a-2-302 (2) GA ST 11-2-302 (3) FL ST 672.302 (4) CO ST 4-2-302 (5) OH ST 1302.15	
Problem Sets K, L, M, N & O	(1) AL ST 6-11-20 (2) NC ST 1D-15 (3) IA ST 668A.1 (4) KY ST 411.186 (5) MN ST 549.20	

1. Briefly describe what the statute provides.

2. Sometimes you will find research notes called annotations following the text of the statute, including summaries of cases that have interpreted the statute. Locate case summaries in the annotations following the statute you retrieved by clicking on the "Notes of Decisions" tab.

Click on the link to any case in the annotations. Provide the name of the case you selected, and briefly describe the case.

II. Lexis Advance

A. Locating Cases in Lexis Advance

Retrieve the same case you retrieved in WestlawNext for Question IA, above. Again, enter only the abbreviated citation to retrieve the case. The citations are repeated below.

To locate a case by citation, enter the abbreviated citation in the Lexis Advance red search box and execute the search. Note that Lexis Advance may display the state reporter citation instead of the regional reporter citation next to the case name.

State Case

Problem Sets A, B, C, D & E	(1) *Winters v. State*, 848 S.W.2d 441
	(2) *Gebhart v. State*, 525 N.E.2d 603
	(3) *Wheeler v. State*, 826 So. 2d 731
	(4) *State v. Gregory*, 869 P.2d 292
	(5) *People v. Toole*, 576 N.W.2d 441
Problem Sets F, G, H, I & J	(1) *Iamartino v. Avallone*, 477 A.2d 124
	(2) *Stefan Jewelers, Inc. v. Electro-Protective Corp.*, 288 S.E.2d 667
	(3) *Credit Alliance Corp. v. Westland Mach. Co., Inc.*, 439 So. 2d 332
	(4) *Davis v. M.L.G. Corp.*, 712 P.2d 985
	(5) *Spectrum Networks, Inc. v. Plus Realty, Cincinnati, Inc.*, 878 N.E.2d 1122
Problem Sets K, L, M, N & O	(1) *Clark v. Kindley*, 10 So. 3d 1005
	(2) *Phillips v. Restaurant Management of Carolina, L.P.*, 552 S.E.2d 686
	(3) *Kuta v. Newberg*, 600 N.W.2d 280
	(4) *Bierman v. Klapheke*, 967 S.W.2d 16
	(5) *Wikert v. Northern Sand and Gravel, Inc.*, 402 N.W.2d 178

1. Briefly describe what the case is about.

2. List at least two format differences you notice between the Lexis and Westlaw versions of this case.

3. After the sections summarizing the decision, you will see a list of LexisNexis Headnotes similar to West headnotes. Read the first headnote and then click on the blue downward arrow next to it. Where does this link take you within the document?

B. Locating Statutes in Lexis Advance

Use Lexis Advance to retrieve a federal statute from its citation.

To locate a statute by citation, enter the abbreviated citation in the red search box and execute the search. Review the search results to locate the correct section. The correct section will ordinarily be the first item in the "Statutes and Legislation" search results.

Federal Statute

Problem Sets A, B, C, D & E	17 uscs 102
	(Retrieve the statutory provision, not the "Revised Title Table.")
Problem Sets F, G, H, I & J	29 uscs 654
Problem Sets K, L, M, N & O	42 uscs 2000a
	(Hint: Be sure to find § 2000a, not 2000(a) or 2000a-1, 2000a-2, etc.)

1. Briefly describe what the statute provides.

2. Sometimes you will find research notes called annotations following the text of the statute, including summaries of cases that have interpreted the statute. Locate case summaries in the annotations following the statute you retrieved. Case summaries appear after the section in the annotations called "Case Notes." You can find this section by scrolling through the document

or by using the option to "Jump to" the Case Notes. Click on any topic in the Case Notes, or scroll past the Case Notes to the case summaries.

Click on the link to any case in the annotations. Provide the name of the case you selected, and briefly describe the case.

Chapter 2
GENERATING SEARCH TERMS

Exercise 2.1
Generating Search Terms

Name: _____   Due Date: _____

Professor: _____   Section: _____

Goal

To learn to generate search terms from a set of facts surrounding a legal question.

Instructions

The charts included in this exercise contain space for you to write. This is for your convenience while you are working on the exercise. After you finish the exercise, you must submit your answers in typewritten form on a separate answer sheet. Do not retype the chart. Submit your answers in the format specified by your professor.

There are no separate problem sets for this exercise.

THE ASSIGNMENT

In legal research, one of the first steps in the research process is generating a list of search terms. You need to use search terms to locate information in a subject index, table of contents, or computer database. This exercise contains charts you can use to generate search terms.

Legal information is often organized by category, so one technique that can help you generate useful search terms is organizing the facts of a legal problem by category. Once you have organized your information by category, you can expand the list to include additional terms. You can expand the list by increasing the breadth and depth of the search terms. You can increase the breadth by brainstorming synonyms or related concepts. You can increase the depth by expressing ideas with varying degrees of abstraction. Here are two examples:

Initial search term	hotel
Terms generated by increasing breadth with synonyms or related terms	motel inn

Initial search term	theft
Terms generated by varying the level of abstraction	robbery (less abstract) crime (more abstract)

The charts that follow list categories of information that can help you generate search terms for effective research. You can use the charts for any of the exercises in this Workbook that require you to generate search terms. You can also use them for other research projects. Several copies of the chart are provided on the following pages.

Chart 1

Categories of information	Initial search terms	Increased breadth (synonyms or related terms)	Increased depth (varying degrees of abstraction)
Parties involved • Describe parties according to their relationships to each other (e.g., landlord and tenant)			
Places and things These can include the following: • Geographic location (e.g., Pennsylvania) • Type of location (e.g., school or church) • Tangible objects (e.g., automobiles) • Intangible concepts (e.g., vacation or reputation)			
Potential claims and defenses If these are not apparent, consider the following: • Parties' conduct (acts done and not done) • Parties' mental states • Injury suffered			
Relief sought by the complaining or injured party			
Additional categories:			

Chart 2

Categories of information	Initial search terms	Increased breadth (synonyms or related terms)	Increased depth (varying degrees of abstraction)
Parties involved • Describe parties according to their relationships to each other (e.g., landlord and tenant)			
Places and things These can include the following: • Geographic location (e.g., Pennsylvania) • Type of location (e.g., school or church) • Tangible objects (e.g., automobiles) • Intangible concepts (e.g., vacation or reputation)			
Potential claims and defenses If these are not apparent, consider the following: • Parties' conduct (acts done and not done) • Parties' mental states • Injury suffered			
Relief sought by the complaining or injured party			
Additional categories:			

Chart 3

Categories of information	Initial search terms	Increased breadth (synonyms or related terms)	Increased depth (varying degrees of abstraction)
Parties involved • Describe parties according to their relationships to each other (e.g., landlord and tenant)			
Places and things These can include the following: • Geographic location (e.g., Pennsylvania) • Type of location (e.g., school or church) • Tangible objects (e.g., automobiles) • Intangible concepts (e.g., vacation or reputation)			
Potential claims and defenses If these are not apparent, consider the following: • Parties' conduct (acts done and not done) • Parties' mental states • Injury suffered			
Relief sought by the complaining or injured party			
Additional categories:			

Chart 4

Categories of information	Initial search terms	Increased breadth (synonyms or related terms)	Increased depth (varying degrees of abstraction)
Parties involved • Describe parties according to their relationships to each other (e.g., landlord and tenant)			
Places and things These can include the following: • Geographic location (e.g., Pennsylvania) • Type of location (e.g., school or church) • Tangible objects (e.g., automobiles) • Intangible concepts (e.g., vacation or reputation)			
Potential claims and defenses If these are not apparent, consider the following: • Parties' conduct (acts done and not done) • Parties' mental states • Injury suffered			
Relief sought by the complaining or injured party			
Additional categories:			

Chart 5

Categories of information	Initial search terms	Increased breadth (synonyms or related terms)	Increased depth (varying degrees of abstraction)
Parties involved • Describe parties according to their relationships to each other (e.g., landlord and tenant)			
Places and things These can include the following: • Geographic location (e.g., Pennsylvania) • Type of location (e.g., school or church) • Tangible objects (e.g., automobiles) • Intangible concepts (e.g., vacation or reputation)			
Potential claims and defenses If these are not apparent, consider the following: • Parties' conduct (acts done and not done) • Parties' mental states • Injury suffered			
Relief sought by the complaining or injured party			
Additional categories:			

Chart 6

Categories of information	Initial search terms	Increased breadth (synonyms or related terms)	Increased depth (varying degrees of abstraction)
Parties involved • Describe parties according to their relationships to each other (e.g., landlord and tenant)			
Places and things These can include the following: • Geographic location (e.g., Pennsylvania) • Type of location (e.g., school or church) • Tangible objects (e.g., automobiles) • Intangible concepts (e.g., vacation or reputation)			
Potential claims and defenses If these are not apparent, consider the following: • Parties' conduct (acts done and not done) • Parties' mental states • Injury suffered			
Relief sought by the complaining or injured party			
Additional categories:			

Chart 7

Categories of information	Initial search terms	Increased breadth (synonyms or related terms)	Increased depth (varying degrees of abstraction)
Parties involved • Describe parties according to their relationships to each other (e.g., landlord and tenant)			
Places and things These can include the following: • Geographic location (e.g., Pennsylvania) • Type of location (e.g., school or church) • Tangible objects (e.g., automobiles) • Intangible concepts (e.g., vacation or reputation)			
Potential claims and defenses If these are not apparent, consider the following: • Parties' conduct (acts done and not done) • Parties' mental states • Injury suffered			
Relief sought by the complaining or injured party			
Additional categories:			

Chart 8

Categories of information	Initial search terms	Increased breadth (synonyms or related terms)	Increased depth (varying degrees of abstraction)
Parties involved • Describe parties according to their relationships to each other (e.g., landlord and tenant)			
Places and things These can include the following: • Geographic location (e.g., Pennsylvania) • Type of location (e.g., school or church) • Tangible objects (e.g., automobiles) • Intangible concepts (e.g., vacation or reputation)			
Potential claims and defenses If these are not apparent, consider the following: • Parties' conduct (acts done and not done) • Parties' mental states • Injury suffered			
Relief sought by the complaining or injured party			
Additional categories:			

Chapter 3
SECONDARY SOURCE RESEARCH

Exercise 3.1
Researching Legal Encyclopedias and A.L.R. Annotations in Print

Name: _____   Due Date: _____

Professor: _____   Section: _____

Goals

1. To use secondary sources to gain background information about a legal issue and to locate citations to primary authorities relevant to the issue.

2. To understand the organization, features, finding tools, and updating tools in legal encyclopedias and A.L.R. Annotations.

Instructions

1. After each question, you will find space to write your answer. This is for your convenience while you are working on the exercise. After you finish your research, submit your answers in typewritten form on a separate answer sheet. Do not retype the questions. Your answer sheet should contain only the answers to the questions.

2. If you spend more than 15 minutes trying to find the answer to any individual question, use the troubleshooting hints in the General Instructions for this Workbook. If you are still unable to find the answer, stop and seek assistance.

3. Reshelve all books as soon as you finish using them.

Problem Set

(circle one)   A   B   C   D   E   F   G   H   I   J   K   L   M   N   O

THE ASSIGNMENT

In this exercise, the supervising attorney in your office has approached you about the client matter for your problem set and has asked you to research it. To do so, you need to research secondary sources to obtain background information and citations to relevant primary authorities. This exercise will guide you through two commonly used secondary sources to obtain the information you need: legal encyclopedias and American Law Reports (A.L.R.) Annotations. As you conduct your research, you will need to answer questions about the information you find in each source.

Review the client matter for your problem set. This client matter involves a complex area of law. Given the complexity of the subject and amount of authority you are likely to find, secondary sources are a good starting point for your research. They will provide you with the background and history of the subject and will refer you to relevant primary authorities.

Part III, the last part in Exercise 3.1, asks you to evaluate when you might use a legal encyclopedia or A.L.R. Annotation. You may want to review Part III before you begin your research so you can consider those questions as you work.

Client Matter

Problem Set A	You represent an insurance company in an automobile injury case. You need to research whether your client's insured may be liable for pain and suffering as a result of the plaintiff's injuries.
Problem Set B	You represent a criminal defendant accused of a non-capital crime. You are seeking bail for your client and need to research the law related to bail.
Problem Set C	You represent a criminal defendant charged with a capital offense, allegedly committed when he was a minor. You need to research law related to capital offenses and criminal punishments.
Problem Set D	You represent a parent in a divorce and custody proceeding. You need to research the law on child custody.
Problem Set E	You represent a popular media Web site that regularly reports on the actions of public officials. You need to research law related to your client's First Amendment rights.
Problem Set F	You are a public prosecutor. You are putting together a case against a local crime ring. You need to research the law of conspiracy.
Problem Set G	You represent another attorney who has been accused of malpractice by a client. You need to research law related to an attorney's duty to his or her client.
Problem Set H	You work in the office of the public defender. Your client received an unusually harsh sentence. You need to research the law of sentences and punishment in order to determine whether you can appeal the harsh sentence.

Problem Set I	You are a public prosecutor. You would like to introduce evidence at trial that was obtained by police officers without a warrant. You need to research law on search and seizure.
Problem Set J	You work for the state legislature. The legislature is considering tort reform and has asked you for legal research on products liability.
Problem Set K	You were recently hired by a law firm that specializes in family law. You need to research law related to divorce.
Problem Set L	You represent a physician who has been accused of medical malpractice. You need to research defenses to medical malpractice claims.
Problem Set M	You work at a law firm that specializes in intellectual property. You need to research law related to patents.
Problem Set N	You represent property owners in a dispute with the local government over its use of eminent domain to take your clients' properties for public use. You need to research the law of eminent domain.
Problem Set O	You work at a plaintiff-side law firm. Your client was injured while visiting a friend's apartment. You need to research law related to a landlord's duty to maintain safe conditions.

I. Legal Encyclopedias

One resource that can be a useful starting point for a research project is a legal encyclopedia. Legal encyclopedias simply report on the state of the law in a very general way. They are helpful for obtaining general background information on your research topic and for locating limited citations to primary legal authority.

A. Locate the legal encyclopedia for your problem set. For Problem Sets A, B, E, F, I, J, and M, go directly to the main encyclopedia volumes. Use the citation provided in your problem set to locate the section of the encyclopedia containing the answers to the questions below. For Problem Sets C, D, G, H, K, L, N, and O, use the subject index to locate the section of the encyclopedia containing the answers to the questions below. Be sure to use the search terms provided in your problem set.

Encyclopedia and Search Terms or Citation

Problem Set A	Am. Jur. 2d	Citation: Damages § 213
Problem Set B	CJS	Citation: Bail § 24
Problem Set C	Am. Jur. 2d	Search Terms: Capital Offenses and Punishment, Cruel and unusual punishment, children and minors
Problem Set D	CJS	Search Terms: Custody of Children, Welfare of child, generally

Problem Set E	Am. Jur. 2d	Citation: Libel and Slander § 42
Problem Set F	CJS	Citation: Conspiracy § 6
Problem Set G	Am. Jur. 2d	Search Terms: Attorney Malpractice, Care and skill, failure to exercise reasonable degree of
Problem Set H	CJS	Search Terms: Sentence and Punishment, Proportionality to offense, generally
Problem Set I	Am. Jur. 2d	Citation: Searches and Seizures § 133
Problem Set J	CJS	Citation: Products Liability § 7
Problem Set K	Am. Jur. 2d	Search Terms: Divorce and Separation, No-fault divorce, generally
Problem Set L	CJS	Search Terms: Medical Malpractice, Defenses
Problem Set M	Am. Jur. 2d	Citation: Patents § 68
Problem Set N	CJS	Search Terms: Eminent Domain, Public use, definition of public use
Problem Set O	Am. Jur. 2d	Search Terms: Premises Liability, Apartments, duty of care

1. For Problem Sets C, D, G, H, K, L, N, and O, provide the topic name and section number you located. For Problem Sets A, B, E, F, I, J, and M, answer "Not Applicable" for this question.

Once you have located the relevant provision for your problem set, answer the legal encyclopedia questions below using the main volume. In question B on page 34, you will use the pocket part to check for updates.

Legal Encyclopedia Questions

Problem Set A	1. According to this section, "pain and suffering" has served as a convenient label under which a plaintiff may recover for what conditions?	2. When may pain and suffering be psychosomatic in origin?
Problem Set B	1. Where a court may exercise discretion with regard to the allowance of bail or the imposition of conditions, what is it proper to consider?	2. What is the consideration that is most pertinent in determining bail?

Problem Set C	1. The Eighth and Fourteenth Amendments prohibit the death penalty for what kind of offenders?	2. Upon what factors did the Supreme Court find evidence of a national consensus against the death penalty for juveniles?
Problem Set D	1. To what extent are past conditions material in determining a parent's right to child custody?	2. What is of prime importance in determining child custody?
Problem Set E	1. What did the United States Supreme Court hold in the case of *New York Times v. Sullivan*?	2. What does actual malice require?
Problem Set F	1. What is a necessary element of a civil conspiracy?	2. What is an "overt act," as the term is used in civil conspiracy proceedings?
Problem Set G	1. An attorney's duty to a client requires him or her to exercise what degree of knowledge, skill, and ability?	2. What must a plaintiff demonstrate in an action to recover damages for legal malpractice?
Problem Set H	1. What should the proportionality analysis be guided by?	2. When may a sentence falling within the statutory range be disturbed on appeal?
Problem Set I	1. According to this section, when is a warrant *not* required for a search under the Fourth Amendment?	2. When do exigent circumstances exist?
Problem Set J	1. Why was strict liability adopted?	2. What idea does strict liability law rest on?
Problem Set K	1. What showing must parties make under no-fault divorce statutes?	2. Why are no-fault divorces also called "conversion" divorces?
Problem Set L	1. Name two matters that may constitute defenses in actions for malpractice.	2. Where a protective and custodial relationship exists, what duty does the caregiver assume?
Problem Set M	1. Who may obtain a patent?	2. According to the relevant legislative history of the patent statute, what did Congress intend the statutory subject matter to include?
Problem Set N	1. How may a "public use" be defined in the law of eminent domain?	2. The term "public use" must be applied in light of two considerations. What are they?
Problem Set O	1. What duty does common law impose on landlords?	2. What two conditions must a plaintiff satisfy in order to establish liability as a result of a statutory violation?

34 Basic Legal Research Workbook

2. Answer the first legal encyclopedia question for your problem set.

3. Answer the second legal encyclopedia question for your problem set.

B. Update your research by checking the pocket part for the main volume. Does the pocket part contain any additional information? If so, provide the name of a case or other resource cited in the pocket part. If not, answer "None." (Hint: Volumes published within the past year will not have pocket parts. If the volume you use is too new to have a pocket part, answer "None.")

II. American Law Reports (A.L.R.) Annotations

American Law Reports, or A.L.R., Annotations collect summaries of cases, typically from a variety of jurisdictions, to provide an overview of the law on a narrow topic. Unlike legal encyclopedias, which usually focus on very broad topics, A.L.R. Annotations tend to focus on narrower legal questions. A.L.R. Annotations are also more detailed than legal encyclopedia entries because they include summaries of specific cases. Like encyclopedia entries, however, they do not contain much analysis. They simply report the results of decisions. A.L.R. Annotations can be a helpful way to begin your legal research to give you an overview of your research topic. They can also direct you to primary authority from the controlling jurisdiction and persuasive authority from other jurisdictions.

Locate the A.L.R. Annotations in your library, and locate an Annotation relevant to the client matter you are researching. For Problem Sets A, B, E, F, I, J, and M, use the A.L.R. Index to locate an Annotation containing the answers to the questions below. Be sure to use the search terms provided in your problem set. For Problem Sets C, D, G, H, K, L, N, and O, go directly to the main A.L.R. volumes. Use the citation provided in your problem set to locate the Annotation containing the answers to the questions below.

A.L.R. Annotation Search Terms or Citation

Problem Set A	Search Terms: Pain and Suffering; Expert and opinion evidence; permanence of injury; generally, necessity of expert testimony on issue of permanence of injury and future pain and suffering
Problem Set B	Search Terms: Bail and Recognizance; Excessive bail; excessiveness of bail in state criminal cases—amounts over $500,000

Problem Set C	Citation: 95 A.L.R.3d 568
Problem Set D	Citation: 26 A.L.R.6th 331
Problem Set E	Search Terms: Libel and Slander; E-mail; individual and corporate liability for libel and slander in electronic communications, including e-mail, Internet and Web sites
Problem Set F	Search Terms: Conspiracy; Corporations; intracorporate conspiracy, construction and application of "intracorporate conspiracy doctrine" as applied to corporation and its employees—state cases
Problem Set G	Citation: 16 A.L.R.6th 653
Problem Set H	Citation: 33 A.L.R.3d 335
Problem Set I	Search Terms: Search and Seizure; Computers; validity of search or seizure of computer, computer disk, or computer peripheral equipment
Problem Set J	Search Terms: Punitive Damages; Statutory cap; construction and application of state statutory cap on punitive damages in tort cases exclusive of medical malpractice actions
Problem Set K	Citation: 55 A.L.R.3d 581
Problem Set L	Citation: 14 A.L.R.6th 301
Problem Set M	Search Terms: Patents; Design, application of ordinary observer test in action for infringement of design patent
Problem Set N	Citation: 21 A.L.R.6th 261
Problem Set O	Citation: 38 A.L.R.4th 240

A. Provide the title of the Annotation you located.

B. Answer the A.L.R. Annotation questions below for your problem set.

A.L.R. Annotation Questions

Problem Set A	1. Using the Article Outline or Index for this Annotation, locate the section dealing with the need for expert testimony regarding "Hearing." Why did the court in *McClure v. Miller* hold that the evidence regarding the plaintiff's injuries was sufficiently objective to enable the jury to make a determination regarding the permanence of his injuries without expert testimony?	2. Locate the "Summary and background—Practice pointers" subsection. How may the nature or persistence of the injury or its effects be shown (without expert testimony)?
Problem Set B	1. Using the Article Outline or Index for this Annotation, locate the section on "Theft crimes—Bail reduced to $500,000 or less." Why did the court in *Mueller v. State* rule that the bail amount of $600,000 was excessive?	2. Locate the subsection on "Practice pointers." Absent any compelling circumstances, to whom should counsel make any application to change bail?
Problem Set C	1. Using the Article Outline for this Annotation, locate the section dealing with "Factors affecting authority; separation of delinquents from adults." What is a commonly found statutory requisite of the incarceration of juveniles?	2. Locate the "Existence or absence of rehabilitative programs" section. What order did the court in *Wilson v. Coughlin* sustain?
Problem Set D	1. Using the Article Outline or Index for this Annotation, locate the section on "Father traveling—Award to mother." Why did the court in *In re Marriage of Stuart* hold that there was no error in awarding custody of the children to the mother?	2. Locate the "Practice Pointers" section. What kinds of testimony can be proof that a custodial parent's residence was seriously inadequate?
Problem Set E	1. Using the Article Outline for this Annotation, locate the portion of the outline on "Defamation Liability Not Found" and "Statement Published on Internet Site." In this portion of the outline, locate the section on "Plaintiff failed to adequately state claim." What did the inmate in *Wells v. Goord* allege?	2. Locate the "Practice Pointers" section. Assuming proper jurisdiction, against whom may a cause of action for defamation on the Internet be brought?

Problem Set F	1. Using the Article Outline or Index for this Annotation, locate the section on the "Scope" of the Annotation. What does the intracorporate conspiracy doctrine hold?	2. Locate the section on "View that intracorporate conspiracy doctrine does not apply to corporate employees acting outside scope of employment." According to *Harp v. King*, what do courts look to in determining whether an employee has acted within the scope of employment?
Problem Set G	1. Using the Article Outline or Index for this Annotation, locate the section on "Summary and comment." What is the so-called "discovery rule"?	2. Locate the "Practice Pointers" section. How has one court described express notice?
Problem Set H	1. Using the Article Outline or Index for this Annotation, locate the section on "Circumstances under which sentence may be cruel and unusual." What kinds of sentences amount to an unconstitutional cruel and unusual punishment?	2. Locate the "Practice Pointers" subsection. What sentencing contingencies should counsel understand and be able to translate to their client?
Problem Set I	1. Using the Article Outline or Index for this Annotation, locate the subsection on "Consent to search or seizure—given by person against whom fruits of search are used—Constitutional violation not established." What argument of the defendant did the court reject in *U.S. v. Roberts*?	2. Locate the subsection on "Summary and comment— Practice pointers." What should practitioners be aware of?
Problem Set J	1. Using the Article Outline or Index for this Annotation, locate the section on "Products liability—Generally." What was the statutory cap on punitive damages in *Sears, Roebuck & Co. v. Kunze*?	2. Locate the section on "Background and summary." What is the purpose of punitive damages?

Problem Set K	1. Using the Article Outline for this Annotation, locate the section on "Construction and effect of provisions setting forth grounds for dissolution of marriage." According to the cases in this section, when should dissolution be decreed? (Hint: Read only the first paragraph of this section.)	2. Locate the "Background and summary: Generally" subsection. What widespread criticism may have contributed to a number of legislatures enacting "no-fault divorce" acts?
Problem Set L	1. Using the Article Outline or Index for this Annotation, locate the section on "Summary and comment." How does this Annotation define a statute of repose?	2. Locate the section on "View that statute begins to run at end of patient's continuous course of treatment—In general." According to *Comstock v. Collier*, what does the statute of repose prevent in cases not covered by exceptions to the statute?
Problem Set M	1. Using the Article Outline or Index for this Annotation, locate the section titled "In general." What is the ordinary observer standard for design patent infringement that the Supreme Court created in *Gorham Mfg. Co. v. White*?	2. Locate the section on "Ordinary observer as interested purchaser." Under *Spotless Enterprises, Inc. v. A&E Products Group L.P.*, who was the ordinary observer?
Problem Set N	1. Using the Article Outline or Index for this Annotation, locate the section on "Background, summary, and comment." What is the general rule, reaffirmed in *Kelo v. City of New London*?	2. Locate the section on "Use-by-public standard." What did the landowners unsuccessfully challenge in *Benson v. State*?
Problem Set O	1. Using the Article Outline or Index for this Annotation, locate the section on "Summary." When have courts been willing to impose liability on a landlord for a physical assault on a tenant by the landlord's employee?	2. Locate the subsection on "Injury to tenant—employee's conduct allegedly within scope of employment—Liability supportable." What did the landlord's agent do in *Sayers v. Boyles* after the tenant told him that he was unable to make the payment demanded by the agent?

1. Answer the first A.L.R. Annotation question for your problem set.

2. Answer the second A.L.R. Annotation question for your problem set.

C. Locate the table listing the jurisdictions from which the Annotation cites authority. How many jurisdictions are listed? (Hint: A.L.R. uses a variety of labels on the table listing jurisdictions. It may be called Table of Jurisdictions Represented, Table of Cases, Jurisdictional Table of Cited Statutes and Cases, or something else to that effect.)

D. Check the pocket part to the main volume to update your research. Does the pocket part list any related A.L.R. Annotations? If so, provide the title of the first Annotation listed. If not, answer "None."

III. Review Questions

A. Would you be most likely to begin your research on a topic about which you knew very little with a legal encyclopedia or an A.L.R. Annotation? Explain your answer.

B. Would you be most likely to use a legal encyclopedia or an A.L.R. Annotation to research the law of multiple jurisdictions? Explain your answer.

C. Which of the following statements is false? (a) C.J.S. and Am. Jur. 2d are national encyclopedias that contain references to cases from across the country; (b) state-specific encyclopedias contain references to cases from an individual state; (c) A.L.R. Annotations address only questions of state law, not federal law.

Exercise 3.2
Researching Secondary Sources Electronically

Name: _____   Due Date: _____

Professor: _____   Section: _____

Goals

1. To use Westlaw, Lexis, and subscription databases to locate secondary sources using table of contents and word searches.

2. To navigate through a secondary source retrieved electronically to locate information within the source.

Instructions

1. After each question, you will find space to write your answer. This is for your convenience while you are working on the exercise. After you finish your research, submit your answers in typewritten form on a separate answer sheet. Do not retype the questions. Your answer sheet should contain only the answers to the questions.

2. If you spend more than 15 minutes trying to find the answer to any individual question, use the troubleshooting hints in the General Instructions for this Workbook. If you are still unable to find the answer, stop and seek assistance.

There are no separate problem sets for this exercise.

THE ASSIGNMENT

A client has come to you with the client matter below, and you need to research this issue.

Six-year-old Reggie Quintal was admitted to Samaritan Hospital for minor surgery to correct an inward deviation of his eyes. The operation was estimated to take 20 minutes. Dr. Palmberg, Reggie's ophthalmologist, was scheduled to perform the procedure; Dr. Thornburg was scheduled to administer the anesthetic.

During the administration of the anesthetic, and before the procedure had been completed, Reggie suffered a respiratory arrest followed by a cardiac arrest, cutting off oxygen to his brain.

Doctors attempted to resuscitate Reggie, and Reggie's heart began again, beating regularly for about four minutes after it stopped. Sometime after the operation, doctors discovered that as a result of lack of oxygen Reggie suffered severe and permanent brain damage.

Reggie's mother asks you whether she can bring a claim for medical malpractice using the doctrine of *res ipsa loquitur*.

Because *res ipsa loquitur* is a doctrine with which you may not be familiar, researching secondary sources would be a good way to begin. The secondary sources you research for this exercise will not provide enough information to answer your client's question. You would need to research primary authority to answer the question. This exercise simply illustrates how secondary sources can be used to obtain background information on a subject and to locate references to primary authority.

For this exercise, you will research secondary sources electronically. Electronic research tools can be very useful in locating secondary sources. Am. Jur. 2d, C.J.S., A.L.R. Annotations, Restatements of the law, many legal periodicals, and some treatises are available electronically. Although electronic tools can be useful for researching secondary sources, they also have some limitations. For example, not all periodicals and only a limited number of treatises are available electronically.

The usefulness of various secondary sources is the same whether you locate them using print or electronic research. Therefore, this exercise will not repeat all the information about secondary sources that appears in Exercise 3.1. Instead, this exercise focuses on electronic search techniques. You can locate secondary sources electronically in a variety of ways. Three common search techniques are: (1) retrieving a document from its citation; (2) browsing a document's table of contents; and (3) executing a word search. Exercise 1.2 covers retrieving authorities from their citations. This exercise illustrates table of contents and word searching.

I. WestlawNext

A. Searching a Legal Encyclopedia Using the Table of Contents

To obtain an overview of the doctrine of *res ipsa loquitur*, you might begin your research with a legal encyclopedia. Both the Am. Jur. 2d and C.J.S. legal encyclopedias are available electronically in Westlaw. Am. Jur. 2d is also available electronically in Lexis. One way to research using a legal encyclopedia is to browse the publication's table of contents.

In WestlawNext, from the "All Content" tab, follow the links to "Secondary Sources," "Texts & Treatises," and "American Jurisprudence 2d." This will bring up the table of contents.

From the main table of contents, one subject that might help with your research into the client matter is "Negligence." From the "Negligence" entry, drill down through each of the following choices to retrieve a section from Am. Jur. 2d:

> Res Ipsa Loquitur
> Introduction
> In General
> Statement of doctrine, generally

1. Review the section of Am. Jur. 2d that you retrieved. Provide the section number.

2. What does *res ipsa loquitur* mean literally?

3. According to the section you retrieved, *res ipsa loquitur* derives from an understanding that some events ordinarily do not occur in the absence of negligence. Provide the name of a New York case that supports that proposition.

   (Hint: In WestlawNext, place the cursor over the footnote number to display the footnote information supporting the textual statement. Use the reporter abbreviations to identify a case decided by a New York (N.Y.) court.)

4. Use the link near the top of the screen to advance to the next section of Am. Jur. 2d. (Hint: Look for the green triangles next to the §.)

   The first paragraph of this section explains what the doctrine of *res ipsa loquitur* is. Briefly explain what showing constitutes sufficient evidence that the injury arose from the defendant's lack of care.

B. Locating A.L.R. Annotations Using Word Searches on WestlawNext

Although most A.L.R. Annotations are also available in Lexis, the first series is not; so WestlawNext should be used on this exercise.

You decide to continue your research on *res ipsa loquitur* in the A.L.R. Annotations in WestlawNext. You are especially interested in learning more details about how *res ipsa loquitur* applies in medical malpractice cases. A.L.R. Annotations are a good place to look for this kind of information.

To answer the questions below, you need to locate the A.L.R. database.

In WestlawNext from the "All Content" tab, follow the links for "Secondary Sources" and "American Law Reports."

Execute the following search:

> Can a physician be held liable for negligence using the doctrine of *res ipsa loquitur*?

1. Review the first 10 items in the search results. Provide the title of the Annotation that seems most relevant to a negligent anesthesia case.

2. Click on the link to open this Annotation. Provide the name of the author of the Annotation.

3. To locate information in an Annotation, you can scroll through the document or use the links to the navigation tools listed in the "Table of Contents" section near the beginning of the document. For this question, use the Article Outline to locate the link to the section discussing "Brain Damage." Provide the names of two cases in which *res ipsa loquitur* was applied when the administration of anesthesia resulted in brain damage.

C. Researching Secondary Sources Using WestlawNext

Using WestlawNext, you can research a variety of secondary sources, including encyclopedias, A.L.R. Annotations, and treatises with a single search. The search results can be limited by jurisdiction, but the search will retrieve many types of authority (statutes, cases, secondary sources, etc.). The advantage to this approach is that it allows you to retrieve multiple forms of authority in a single search. When you are not sure what type of authority will help you answer a research question or when you know you need multiple types of authority, a global search can be effective. The disadvantage is that having all results in a single search may make it difficult to focus on the most relevant or most authoritative sources. You must evaluate the results carefully to make sure you locate and use the best authority available to resolve your research issue.

To continue your research into secondary sources that discuss *res ipsa loquitur*, enter the following search in the WestlawNext global search box:

res ipsa loquitur and medical malpractice

(Hint: If you have just completed Section A or B of this part of the exercise you may see tabs above the global search box. If so, click on the "All Content" tab and select "All States" and "All Federal" in the jurisdiction selection box before executing the search.)

1. Using the filtering options under "View," display the "Secondary Sources" results. Using the additional filtering options, limit the "Publication Type" to ALR. (Hint: After checking the box for "ALR," you may need to click "Apply Filters.") This will limit the display to A.L.R. Annotations. Review the search results. (Notice that the annotation relating to negligent anesthesia cases that you located for Question B1, above, also appears in these search results.) Provide the title of an annotation on *res ipsa loquitur* claims against hospitals.

2. Because WestlawNext aggregates sources in the search results, you can also find treatise entries on the subject you are researching. Using the filtering options, undo the filter limiting the display to A.L.R. Annotations, and scroll down to select the option to "Select a Publication Name." From the list, enter or select "Modern Tort Law: Liability and Litigation" and apply it as the filter. Review the filtered search results, and locate a section of the treatise that deals with "Res Ipsa Loquitur—Application to particular cases—Medical malpractice cases." Review the section of the treatise, and answer the following questions:

    a. In medical malpractice actions, the doctrine of *res ipsa loquitur* has been applied in five situations. List the five situations.

    b. Some jurisdictions have limited the application of *res ipsa loquitur* in medical malpractice cases. Give one such limitation.

II. Lexis

A. Locating Legal Periodicals Using Word Searches in Lexis Advance

Although this question directs you to use Lexis, you can also locate legal periodicals in Westlaw.

The material you have located so far provides some information about *res ipsa loquitur*, but you clearly need more. You decide to research legal periodicals to learn more. In particular, you want to learn more about problems in applying *res ipsa loquitur* to medical malpractice cases.

One way to locate legal periodicals is through word searches. To do so you will first want to narrow the scope of the search to Secondary Materials. Go to the main Lexis Advance search screen, and set the filter for "Secondary Materials" (in the "Category" tab). After setting a filter for Secondary Materials, search for:

> res ipsa loquitur and medical malpractice

Narrow those search results to only Law Reviews and Journals. (Hint: Use the "Narrow By" menu, and click "Law Reviews and Journals" under "Category.")

1. Browse the search results, and locate a 1996 note in the University of Virginia Law Review. Provide the title of the article.

2. Click on the link to the article you located for Question A1, above, to view the full text of the article. Locate the section of the article discussing Evolution and then the subsection discussing Res Ipsa Loquitur and Medical Malpractice Actions. Give three reasons why it was difficult to prove the first prong of the *res ipsa loquitur* doctrine and thus why the doctrine initially was not applicable to medical malpractice cases.

B. Locating Restatements of the Law Using Word Searches in Lexis Advance

Although this question directs you to use Lexis, you can also locate Restatements in Westlaw.

You would like to continue your research into the problems applying *res ipsa loquitur* in medical malpractice cases. You decide to research Restatements to see if they offer any new information.

Browse Sources by clicking the "Browse" button near the top of the screen and clicking "Sources." Click "By Category" and "Secondary Materials." Search for "Restatement of the Law 2d Torts – Rule Sections," using the "Search for a source" box. Click on "Restatement of Law 2d Torts – Rule Sections," and add this source as a filter. Now execute the following search:

> res ipsa loquitur and medical malpractice

1. Provide the number of the Restatement section that discusses *res ipsa loquitur*.

2. Click on the link for this Restatement section. When you conduct a word search, one way to locate relevant information within a document is by using the "Jump To" function to Navigate to your search terms. The "Term" function, which is available in both Lexis and Westlaw, allows you to jump to the portion of the document where the search terms appear. To use this function, click on the "Jump To" arrow at the top of the screen and under "Navigate" you can jump to the search terms.

   Use the "Navigate" function to search for the terms "res ipsa loquitur" until you see the sentence: "To such events res ipsa loquitur may apply." Following that sentence is the section of the document titled "Basis of conclusion." Give an example of a kind of medical malpractice case where no expert is needed to tell the jury that such events do not usually occur in the absence of negligence.

C. Researching Other Secondary Sources in Lexis Advance

The red search box in Lexis Advance allows you to search all content without specifying a database. As you have just seen, the search results can be limited by type of authority, jurisdiction, or practice area or topic. Without these limits, however, the search will retrieve many types of authority (statutes, cases, secondary sources, etc.).

Continue your research on *res ipsa loquitur* and the need for expert testimony. From the red search box limit the "Category" to "Secondary Materials." (Hint: Be sure to delete any other "Narrow By" filters.) Enter the following search in the red search box:

res ipsa loquitur expert testimony

1. Use the narrowing options to view Expert Analysis documents. (Hint: Look in the "Category" tab.) Locate a document by David Fish regarding the need for expert testimony in a *res ipsa loquitur* case. Provide the title of the document, and briefly describe the facts of the case that is the focus of the article.

2. Return to the search results list. View the Web results the search retrieved. Click on the link to one of the sites in the search results, and review the content. Provide the name of the site you selected. Is the site you viewed a source you would cite in a legal document? Explain why or why not.

48 Basic Legal Research Workbook

III. Subscription Databases for Legal Periodicals

Having examined several secondary sources, you now would like to research the most recent scholarly writing on *res ipsa loquitur*. Law review articles are a good place to look for the latest writing on a topic like *res ipsa loquitur*.

You can use Westlaw and Lexis to locate law review articles (just as you located other secondary sources above). You can also use subscription services available through your law school library to locate law review articles. Popular subscription services include HeinOnline, LegalTrac, and the Index to Legal Periodicals (or "ILP"). This exercise directs you to use the ILP. LegalTrac may be used if your library does not subscribe to ILP.

From your library's Web site, locate the Index to Legal Periodicals. (Hint: If you have access to more than one database, choose Index to Legal Periodicals – Full Text.) Click on the link to the Index to Legal Periodicals or follow any other instructions on your library's Web site to access the service. Choose the option for "Advanced Search." Under "Limit your results," limit the dates to from January to December 2009. Enter the following search phrase in the first search box as a Text search:

res ipsa loquitur

Execute the search by clicking the "Search" button. Find a 2009 article in the Wake Forest Law Review. Click on the Full Text PDF, and answer the following questions.

A. Provide the name of the article.

B. According to the article, what common theme do the doctrines of negligence per se and *res ipsa loquitur* share?

C. According to the article, how would the *Restatement (Third) of Torts* be more effective and more principled?

Exercise 3.3
Researching Secondary Sources on Your Own

Name: _____ Due Date: _____

Professor: _____ Section: _____

Goals

1. To locate a secondary source on a specific area of law to gain information about a legal issue.
2. To use a secondary source to identify primary authority.

Instructions

1. After each question, you will find space to write your answer. This is for your convenience while you are working on the exercise. After you finish your research, submit your answers in typewritten form on a separate answer sheet. Do not retype the questions. Your answer sheet should contain only the answers to the questions.

2. If you spend more than 15 minutes trying to find the answer to any individual question, use the troubleshooting hints in the General Instructions for this Workbook. If you are still unable to find the answer, stop and seek assistance.

Problem Set

(circle one)   A   B   C   D   E   F

THE ASSIGNMENT

For this exercise, assume that the supervising attorney in your office has asked you to research the client matter set out in your problem set. This client matter involves an area of the law that may be new or unfamiliar to you. Consequently, secondary sources are a good starting point for your research.

Using WestlawNext or Lexis Advance, research any secondary source(s) to find the answers to the questions for your problem set.

Client Matter and Legal Question

Problem Set A	**Client Matter:** You work in a prosecutor's office. Your office is considering bringing charges against several individuals in a local crime ring for criminal conspiracy. You need to research the elements of criminal conspiracy.	**Legal Question:** What are the elements, or what is the definition, of criminal conspiracy (at common law, or in any jurisdiction)?
Problem Set B	**Client Matter:** Your client wishes to evict a squatter, but she is worried that the squatter may have acquired rights to a portion of her property. You need to research the law of adverse possession.	**Legal Question:** What are the elements, or what is the definition, of adverse possession (at common law, or in any jurisdiction)?
Problem Set C	**Client Matter:** Your client wishes to contest a portion of a contract by introducing statements made by a party to the contract before the contract was signed. You need to research the parol evidence rule.	**Legal Question:** What is the parol (or extrinsic) evidence rule (at common law, or in any jurisdiction)?
Problem Set D	**Client Matter:** Your client injured another person in a car accident. The injured person suffered unusually severe injuries due to a preexisting condition. You need to research the "eggshell skull" doctrine in tort.	**Legal Question:** What is the eggshell skull (or thin skull, or preexisting conditions) doctrine?
Problem Set E	**Client Matter:** Your client is charged with commission of a crime. You think your client may be not guilty by reason of insanity. You need to research the insanity defense in criminal law.	**Legal Question:** What must you show to succeed in your insanity defense (at common law, or in any jurisdiction)?
Problem Set F	**Client Matter:** Your client owns a swimming pool on her private property. Recently a neighborhood child was injured while swimming in the pool without your client's permission. The child's parents are threatening to sue. You need to research the attractive nuisance doctrine in tort.	**Legal Question:** What is the attractive nuisance (or "infant trespasser" or "turntable") doctrine (at common law, or in any jurisdiction)?

I. Provide the name and citation of at least one, but no more than three, secondary sources you consulted to find the answer to the legal question. Describe how you located each source.

II. Answer the legal question.

III. Provide the name and citation of at least one, but no more than three, primary authorities cited in the secondary source(s) you consulted that support your answer to Question II, above.

Chapter 4
CASE RESEARCH

Exercise 4.1
Researching Cases in Print

Name: _____   Due Date: _____

Professor: _____   Section: _____

Goals

1. To become familiar with the coverage and organization of digests.
2. To locate case summaries in a print digest using the headnotes in a case on point and the Descriptive-Word Index.
3. To review the topic outline at the beginning of a digest topic to locate relevant Key Numbers.
4. To update print digest research using pocket parts and supplements.

Instructions

1. After each question, you will find space to write your answer. This is for your convenience while you are working on the exercise. After you finish your research, submit your answers in typewritten form on a separate answer sheet. Do not retype the questions. Your answer sheet should contain only the answers to the questions.

2. If you spend more than 15 minutes trying to find the answer to any individual question, use the troubleshooting hints in the General Instructions for this Workbook. If you are still unable to find the answer, stop and seek assistance.

3. Although some questions include hints reminding you to update your research, others do not. Do not forget to update your research in all sources even if the question does not prompt you to do so.

4. Reshelve all books as soon as you finish using them.

Problem Set

(circle one)   A B C D E F G H I J K L M N O P Q R

THE ASSIGNMENT

One way to locate cases is to search by subject, and the West digest system is the most commonly used resource for researching cases by subject in print. For this part of the exercise you must use West reporters and digests.

This exercise presents two issues for you to research using digests. The first issue requires you to use a case on point as a vehicle for locating digest summaries of additional cases relevant to your research. The second issue requires you to use the digest index to locate cases. This exercise will guide you through the research process. As you conduct your research, you will need to provide answers to the legal question for your problem set. Answer the questions using the cases you locate; do not conduct additional research.

I. Review Questions

A. Explain the difference between a digest and a reporter.

B. List two digests that would include a summary of *Frank v. City of Akron*, 95 F. Supp. 2d 706 (N.D. Ohio 1999).

C. Digest case summaries begin with information about the court that decided the case. The court information can help you focus on summaries most relevant to your research, especially when you are using a digest set summarizing cases from more than one jurisdiction. The three court abbreviations below are typical of those that appear in digests. Review the abbreviations and provide the information requested.

    C.A.6 (Mich.)   W.D. Mich.   Mich.

1. Which of these abbreviations refers to a federal court? Provide the level(s) of the court(s) indicated by the abbreviation(s).

2. Which of these abbreviations refers to a state court? Provide the level(s) of the court(s) indicated by the abbreviation(s).

II. Working from a Case on Point

One way to use the digest for case research is to work from a case on point. The West digest topics and Key Numbers are consistent across jurisdictions. Therefore, once you have located a case on point from any jurisdiction, you can use that case as an entry point into the West digest system to research cases from any other jurisdiction.

Your client has approached you about the following situation:

> Your client, Mitch Cortez, and Stephanie Morgan had been living together since 2004. Although they had not participated in a formal marriage ceremony, they referred to each other as husband and wife, and their family and friends treated them as a married couple. When they moved in together, they decided to buy a house. Mr. Cortez could qualify for a mortgage on favorable terms, but Ms. Morgan could not. Therefore, they decided to put the house and mortgage in Mr. Cortez's name only. Mr. Cortez paid the down payment from money he had saved. They paid the monthly mortgage payments and other living expenses from a joint checking account into which both of them contributed funds. Mr. Cortez repeatedly promised Ms. Morgan that he would retitle the property in both names, but he never did. Six months ago, the parties ended their relationship. Ms. Morgan now claims that she is a half-owner of the house. Mr. Cortez claims he is the sole owner. Mr. Cortez has asked you to find out whether Ms. Morgan has a valid claim to a half-share of the property under the law of the jurisdiction for your problem set.

A. Review the legal question and identify the jurisdiction for your problem set.

Jurisdiction and Legal Question

Jurisdiction	Legal Question
Problem Set A (Kansas)	One possible issue in the parties' situation is whether they formed a common-law marriage by living together and holding themselves out as a married couple. What are the requirements of a common-law marriage in the jurisdiction for your problem set?
Problem Set B (Texas)	
Problem Set C (Alabama)	
Problem Set D (Oklahoma)	
Problem Set E (Ohio)	
Problem Set F (jurisdiction assigned by your professor)	

Jurisdiction	Legal Question
Problem Set G (Arizona)	One possible issue in the parties' situation is the effect of Mr. Cortez's promise to retitle the house in both parties' names. This promise did not form an enforceable contract. A doctrine called "promissory estoppel" or "detrimental reliance" sometimes allows a person to enforce an oral promise that does not qualify as an enforceable contract. What must a plaintiff show to establish a promissory estoppel or detrimental reliance claim in the jurisdiction for your problem set?
Problem Set H (South Carolina)	
Problem Set I (Illinois)	
Problem Set J (Florida)	
Problem Set K (Minnesota)	
Problem Set L (jurisdiction assigned by your professor)	

Jurisdiction	Legal Question
Problem Set M (Maryland)	One possible issue in the parties' situation is whether Mr. Cortez will be unjustly enriched by retaining sole ownership of the house. What are the elements of an unjust enrichment claim (sometimes called an implied, quasi, or constructive contract claim) in the jurisdiction for your problem set?
Problem Set N (Wisconsin)	
Problem Set O (Pennsylvania)	
Problem Set P (Utah)	
Problem Set Q (Missouri)	
Problem Set R (jurisdiction assigned by your professor)	

Assume that you began your research on this question by reviewing secondary sources and that one of the secondary sources referenced the case listed below for your problem set, which is from another jurisdiction. You can use the topics and Key Numbers in the headnotes from the case listed below to identify similar cases from the jurisdiction for your problem set.

Case On Point

Problem Set	Case On Point
A-F	*Hurley v. Hurley*, 721 P.2d 1279 (Mont. 1986) (discussing the *requisites* for a *common-law marriage*)
G-L	*1861 Group, L.L.C. v. Wild Oats Markets, Inc.*, 728 F. Supp. 2d 1052 (E.D. Mo. 2010) (describing the *elements* of a *promissory estoppel* claim)
M-R	*Jackson-Jester v. Aziz*, 48 So. 3d 88 (Fla. Dist. Ct. App. 2010) (describing the *elements* of an *unjust enrichment* claim)

Look up the case provided, and review the headnotes at the beginning of the case. Use the headnotes to identify a topic and accompanying Key Number related to the legal question for your problem set.

Provide the topic and Key Number that seem most relevant to the legal question.

(Hint: Often, multiple topics or Key Numbers will be relevant to an issue you are researching. To research the legal question for your problem set fully, you might research cases under several topics and Key Numbers. This question requires you to identify only one topic and Key Number. Use the terms in italics as a guide to identify the appropriate topic and Key Number for your problem set.)

B. Locate the most current series of a digest that summarizes cases from the jurisdiction for your problem set. This may be a state-specific digest or a regional digest, depending on the jurisdiction and your library's holdings.

Provide the name and, if appropriate, series (e.g., 2d, 3d, 4th) of the digest you used.

C. You can locate relevant case summaries by looking up the topic and Key Number you listed for Question IIA, above, in the digest containing summaries of cases from the jurisdiction for your problem set.

Look up the topic and Key Number in the main digest volumes, and review the case summaries. Then do the same in the pocket part or cumulative supplement. (Hints: The pocket part may or may not list cases from the jurisdiction from your problem set. Main digest volumes that have been reprinted recently may not have pocket parts or cumulative supplements.)

1. Provide the name and citation (as they appear in the digest) for at least two, but no more than three, cases from the state courts in the jurisdiction for your problem set that answer the legal question.

    (Hints: Focus on cases decided by the state courts in the jurisdiction for your problem set. Regional digests may list cases from multiple states. State digests may list federal cases before cases decided by the state's courts. Look for case summaries that list or describe the items necessary to establish the claim for your problem set. If the digest lists more than one citation for the case (e.g., citations for denials of rehearing or *certiorari*), provide only the first citation.)

    (Hint for Problem Sets F, L, and R: The case summaries may not list elements but may instead simply describe the requirements in general terms.)

2. Were any of the cases you listed for Question C1, above, summarized in the pocket part or cumulative supplement? If so, list the case(s). If not, answer "no."

D. Cases with helpful information on your research issue may appear under related Key Numbers within the same topic. Each digest topic has a topic outline at the beginning of the topic in the main volume of the digest. The topic outline can be useful for identifying additional Key Numbers relevant to your research. Turn back to the topic outline at the beginning of your topic in the main digest volume, and locate the Key Number indicated for your problem set.

Key Number

Problem Sets A-F	Marriage by cohabitation and reputation
Problem Sets G-L	Relying and acting on representations
Problem Sets M-R	Use and occupation of realty

E. Look up one case you listed for Question IIC, above, in the appropriate reporter.

1. Briefly describe the facts of the case. (Hint: If the case is long, focus on the facts relevant to the legal question you are researching.)

2. Using only this case, answer the legal question for your problem set. The headnotes will help you identify the portion of the case relevant to the legal question.

3. Using only this case, explain briefly whether the requirements or elements you listed above likely can be satisfied in this case. (Hint: You may not be able to reach a definitive conclusion using only the facts provided. Make your best assessment using the information you have.)

III. Using the Descriptive-Word Index

You do not have to locate a case on point to access the digest. You can also use the Descriptive Word Index to find relevant topics and Key Numbers. Assume you learned the following new facts about your client's situation:

Mr. Cortez had promised to marry Ms. Morgan, and Ms. Morgan had begun wedding planning when the parties ended their relationship. Ms. Morgan is threatening to file an action for breach of a promise to marry against Mr. Cortez for calling off the wedding. You need to find out whether a claim for a broken marriage promise would be valid in the jurisdiction for your problem set.

A. Locate the Descriptive Word Index for the digest set you used for Part II, above. Look up "Breach of Marriage Promise." (Hint for Problem Sets F, L, and R: You may need to look up additional or different terms to find a topic relevant to the legal question.)

Review the index entries. You should see a variety of subheadings, most or all of which refer to a single topic. To which topic do the index entries refer you?

B. Look up the topic you identified for Question A, above, in the digest. Review the topic outline. Which Key Number summarizes cases relating to defenses to an action for breach of a promise to marry?

C. Review the case summaries under the topic, and answer the digest question below for your problem set. (Hint: More than one case may apply. You only need to list one case to answer the question.)

Digest Question

Problem Set	Question
A	**If you are using the state digest:** Provide the name of a state case that discusses the circumstances under which pregnancy may be proved and considered in an action for breach of promise.
	If you are using the regional digest: Provide the name of the most recent state case from *any* state in the region.
B	Provide the name of a state case that explains that the state's equal rights amendment did not abolish the common-law breach of marriage promise action.
C	Provide the name of a state case that discusses a statute that abolishes civil actions for breach of a promise to marry.
D	Provide the name of a state case that discusses the effect of fraud on consent to a marriage agreement.
E	Provide the name of a state case that explains that an action for emotional distress arising out of a broken marriage promise is an amatory action.
F	Answer the question provided by your professor.
G	**If you are using the state digest:** Provide the name of a state case that explains that the question of whether the plaintiff knew the defendant was married when he proposed to her was for the jury.
	If you are using the regional digest: Provide the name of the most recent state case from *any* state in the region.
H	Provide the name of a state case that explains that a breach of marriage promise action remains viable.
I	Provide the name of a *federal* case that discusses the effect of the Breach of Promise Act on a common-law action for breach of marriage promise.
J	Provide the name of a state case that discusses a statute that abolishes actions for breach of a contract to marry.

K	Provide the name of a state case that discusses a statute that abolished civil actions for breach of promises to marry.
L	Answer the question provided by your professor.
M	Provide the name of a state case that discusses a statute abolishing remedies for breach of promise to marry.
N	Provide the name of a state case that explains that a girlfriend cannot maintain an unjust enrichment claim against her boyfriend based on housekeeping contributions made in contemplation of marriage.
O	Provide the name of a state case that explains that the Heart Balm Act prohibits a claim for money spent in reliance on an unfulfilled promise to marry.
P	Provide the name of a state case that explains that an action for breach of a promise to marry cannot be maintained.
Q	Provide the name of a state case that discusses whether it was proper to instruct the jury about the alteration of the plaintiff's moral and social standing as an element of damages in a breach of marriage promise case.
R	Answer the question provided by your professor.

Exercise 4.2
Researching Cases Electronically

Name: _____   Due Date: _____

Professor: _____   Section: _____

Goals

1. To research cases electronically by subject.
2. To research cases electronically using word searches.

Instructions

1. After each question, you will find space to write your answer. This is for your convenience while you are working on the exercise. After you finish your research, submit your answers in typewritten form on a separate answer sheet. Do not retype the questions. Your answer sheet should contain only the answers to the questions.

2. If you spend more than 15 minutes trying to find the answer to any individual question, use the troubleshooting hints in the General Instructions for this Workbook. If you are still unable to find the answer, stop and seek assistance.

There are no separate problem sets for this exercise.

THE ASSIGNMENT

This exercise is related to Exercise 4.1, Researching Cases in Print. You do not have to complete Exercise 4.1, however, before completing this exercise. For this exercise, you will conduct your research using electronic resources. You can research cases electronically in a variety of ways. Three common search techniques are: (1) retrieving a case from its citation; (2) searching by subject area; and (3) executing a word search. Exercise 1.2, Introduction to Electronic Research, illustrates how to retrieve a case from its citation. This exercise focuses on searching by subject area and word searching.

When you retrieve cases electronically, often you will see symbols next to the case citations, including red or yellow flags in Westlaw and red stop signs or yellow triangles in Lexis. You will learn about these symbols when you learn about a research tool called a citator. In this Workbook, citators are covered in Chapter 5, Research with Citators.

I. Review Questions

A. Are headnotes added by publishers at the beginning of a case ever authoritative?

B. Assume you located a case reported in F.3d. Which of the following statements about this case is true? (1) The case was decided by a federal court. (2) The case was decided by a trial court. (3) The case was decided by a state court.

C. Assume you located a case reported in Fed. Appx. Which of the following statements about this case is false? (1) The case was decided by a federal court. (2) The case was decided by a trial court. (3) The case is nonprecedential.

II. Legal Question

Your client has come to you with the following problem:

Your client, Mitch Cortez, and Stephanie Morgan had been living together since 2004. Although they had not participated in a formal marriage ceremony, they referred to each other as husband and wife, and their family and friends treated them as a married couple. When they moved in together, they decided to buy a house. Mr. Cortez could qualify for a mortgage on favorable terms, but Ms. Morgan could not. Therefore, they decided to put the house and mortgage in Mr. Cortez's name only. Mr. Cortez paid the down payment from money he had saved. They paid the monthly mortgage payments and other living expenses from a joint checking account into which they both contributed funds. Mr. Cortez repeatedly promised Ms. Morgan that he would retitle the property in both names, but he never did. Six months ago, the parties ended their relationship. Ms. Morgan now claims that she is a half-owner of the house. Mr. Cortez claims he is the sole owner. Mr. Cortez has asked you to find out whether Ms. Morgan has a valid claim to a half-share of the property.

One possible claim Ms. Morgan may raise is that the court should create a constructive trust to convey an interest in the property to her. You need to research the law of constructive trust to see whether Ms. Morgan is likely to prevail with this claim.

III. WestlawNext

A. Searching by Subject Using Topics and Key Numbers

In WestlawNext, you can search by subject using topics and Key Numbers. Because topics and Key Numbers are proprietary West editorial features, you can conduct topic and Key Number searches only in Westlaw.

You can browse the West Key Number System in WestlawNext if you know which topic you want to search. You can also access digest topics and Key Numbers from a case on point, much as you would in print. You can find cases on point in a variety of ways, including through secondary sources. Assume that you found the citation to the following case in a legal encyclopedia:

Bergmann v. Slater, 922 So. 2d 1110 (Fla. Dist. Ct. App. 2006).

Retrieve this case in WestlawNext, and review the headnotes at the beginning of the opinion. Each headnote is assigned at least one topic and Key Number subdivision, and you can use the link to the Key Number to locate additional cases on the same topic. For purposes of your research on constructive trusts, headnote 7 has the most relevant information.

WestlawNext displays headnotes in two ways. Next to headnote 7 is a link to Trusts. This link is followed by a key symbol and a link to Nature of Constructive Trust. (Hint: If you see a list of subjects accompanied by hyperlinked numbers in a box to the right of the headnote, use the "Change View" link above headnote 1.)

Click on the link to "Nature of Constructive Trust." This will bring up a list of Florida and related federal cases summarized under the Trusts topic, Nature of Constructive Trust Key Number. (By way of explanation, at the top of the results, you will see the topic "390 Trusts" followed by an outline of subdivisions. The link to 390 [key symbol] 91 refers to the topic Trusts (390) and the Key Number subdivision 91 (Nature of Constructive Trust).) The list of case summaries is similar to those you would see in the print digest if you looked up the topic and Key Number.

To narrow your search results, type "fraud" in the box labeled "Search within results" on the left. Apply the filter.

1. Review the case summaries your search retrieved. Provide the names and citations (as they appear in the results list) of three cases decided by Florida state courts that explain when a constructive trust can be imposed on a property even though the property was not acquired by fraud.

   (Hints: More than three cases may apply. You only need to list three cases to answer this question. The results include related federal cases. Be sure to locate state cases to answer this question. To limit the results to Florida state cases, change the jurisdiction to eliminate related federal cases, and re-execute the search.)

2. Locate a summary of a case decided in August 2000 by the Third District Court of Appeal. Click on the link to the case, and review the opinion. Provide the name of the case, and briefly explain why this case presented an unusual factual scenario.

B. Word Searching

Word searching is another way to locate cases. The global search box in WestlawNext allows you to search all content without specifying a database. The search results can be limited by jurisdiction, but the search will retrieve many types of authority (statutes, cases, secondary sources, etc.). The advantage to this approach is that it allows you to retrieve multiple forms of authority in a single search. When you are not sure which type of authority will help you answer a research question, or when you know you need multiple types of authority, a global search can be effective. The disadvantage is that having all results in a single search may make it difficult to focus on the most relevant or most authoritative sources. You must evaluate the results carefully to make sure you locate and use the best authority available to resolve your research issue.

Continue your research into Ms. Morgan's potential constructive trust claim by using WestlawNext to determine the strength of the evidence necessary to establish the right to a constructive trust.

Locate the global search box. Use the jurisdiction selection box next to the search box to limit the jurisdiction to Florida. (Hint: Check the box for Florida and uncheck all other boxes. Click on the "All Content" tab before executing the search.)

Enter the following search in the global search box:

constructive trust proof

Execute the search, and review the search results. Notice that it retrieves thousands of documents organized by document type. Review the case results in the "Cases" tab. Sort the results by Relevance.

1. Use the filtering options to restrict the results to cases decided by the Supreme Court of Florida. (Hint: Filtering options are available in the "Narrow" menu on the left side of the screen. Scroll down to the Jurisdiction option, and drill down through the menu options to select Florida Supreme Ct.)

   To determine the standard of proof necessary to establish the right to a constructive trust, review the summaries of the first 10 cases in the search results and view the full text of the cases as necessary. Based on your research, how strong must the proof or evidence be to establish a constructive trust? Cite a case which supports your conclusion. (Hint: The search will retrieve more than 10 cases. Review no more than 10 cases to answer this question.)

2. Review the search results to locate a 1959 case that concerns a meretricious relationship, and view the full text of the case. Provide the name of the case and citation, and briefly explain why, although compelled by precedent to reverse the Chancellor's decree, the court did so reluctantly. (Hint: You can locate the case by reviewing the case summaries in the search results or by searching within the search results for the term "meretricious.")

IV. Lexis Advance

A. Word Searching

To continue the research into Ms. Morgan's potential constructive trust claim, it would be helpful to evaluate Florida cases specifically addressing constructive trust claims by unmarried cohabitants.

The red search box in Lexis Advance allows you to search all content without specifying a database. The search results can be limited by type of authority, jurisdiction, practice area, or topic. Without these limits, however, the search will retrieve many types of authority (statutes, cases, secondary sources, etc.). The advantage to this approach is that it allows you to retrieve multiple forms of authority in a single search. When you are not sure what type of authority will help you answer a research question, or when you know you need multiple types of authority, a global search can be effective. The disadvantage is that having all results in a single search may make it difficult to focus on the most relevant or most authoritative sources. You must evaluate the results carefully to make sure you locate and use the best authority available to resolve your research issue.

Limit your search to Florida state cases. (Hint: Click on "Filters." Now click on "Jurisdiction," and select "Florida." Click on "Category," and select "Cases.") Execute the following search:

constructive trust and unmarried cohabitants

Review the search results.

1. Provide the name and citation of a case decided by the Second District Court of Appeal in 1993 that addresses a claim against a live-in partner for services performed in the partner's business.

2. Review the case. The appellate court concluded that the trial court erred when it decided that case. What was the trial court's error?

B. Searching by Subject Using Topics and Headnotes

Although the West topics and Key Numbers are unique to Westlaw, LexisNexis has its own subject searching tools. You can browse a list of topics by choosing the option to browse topics from the "Browse" menu at the top of the page. You can also use the headnotes in a case on point to search by subject.

Return to the case you identified for Question A, above. At the beginning of the case, you will find a list of subject areas that categorizes the case and a LexisNexis Headnote that quotes language from the case. From the list of subject areas, locate the subject "Estate, Gift & Trust Law," and click on the

"Constructive Trusts" sub-topic. Click "Get documents." Using the "Narrow By" filters on the left side of the screen, narrow your search by jurisdiction to Florida.

Provide the names and citations (as they appear in the search results) of two additional cases that involve constructive trust claims arising out of boyfriend/girlfriend relationships. (Hints: Narrow your results by typing "boyfriend" in the "Search Within Results" box. Do not use the case you used to answer Question A, above, in the answer; list two *additional* cases. More than two additional cases may involve boyfriend/girlfriend relationships. You only need to list two cases to answer this question.)

C. Using the filtering options, continue your research into Ms. Morgan's potential constructive trust claim. One basis for imposition of a constructive trust is abuse of a confidential relationship. You need to research whether Ms. Morgan and Mr. Cortez had a confidential relationship.

Go back to the main Lexis Advance search page, and locate the red search box. (Hint: Click "Lexis Advance Research" in the upper-left corner of the page.) Use the "Filter" menus to select Florida as the jurisdiction; do not limit the categories. (Hint: Check the box for Florida in "Jurisdiction." Uncheck the box for "Cases" in "Category." Alternatively, you can de-select "Cases" from the "Narrow By" options.)

Enter the following search in the red search box:

constructive trust and confidential relationship

Execute the search, and review the search results. Notice that it retrieves multiple types of authority organized under tabs by document type.

1. Review the results under the "Cases" tab. The results are listed by relevance. To change the order to display Florida Supreme Court cases first, click on "Supreme Court" under "Court" in the "Narrow By" options, or use the "Sort by" option in the top right corner to sort by "Court (highest - lowest)." Provide the name and citation of a Florida Supreme Court case from 1955.

2. Turn off the Supreme Court filter so you have all Florida state cases. Use the filtering options to narrow the results by the Keyword "confidential relationship." (Hint: Find the "Keyword" option in the "Narrow By" menu on the left side of the screen. Click on "more" to view the complete list of Keywords.)

    To determine when parties are in a confidential relationship, review the summaries of the first 10 cases in the search results and view the full text of the cases as necessary. Based on your research, when is a confidential relationship found? Cite a case which supports your conclusion. (Hint: The search may retrieve more than 10 cases. Review no more than 10 cases to answer this question.)

3. Remove the filter for keyword "confidential relationship." (Hint: Click the "x" next to "confidential relationship" under the "Narrow By" options that you have selected.) Review the search results to locate a 1965 case that concerns a claim by a decedent's mistress, and view the full text of the case. Provide the name and citation of the case, and briefly explain why the order dismissing the complaint was reversed.

4. Lexis Advance has a unique search feature called Legal Issue Trail searching, a form of subject searching. This feature allows you to use specific passages within a case to locate similar cases.

    Viewing the full text of the case you located for Question 3, above, you will see a link to Legal Issue Trail in the right margin. Click on the link to "Activate Passages." Locate the first passage identified in the text. (Hint: Identified passages are outlined. The first passage indicates, among other things, that the "origin of the confidence is immaterial.")

    Click on the first passage identified to bring up a list of cases that have cited the case you originally located for the issue addressed in the passage. (Hint: Click on the text, and not the case citation, in the outlined box.)

    Click on the link to a 1993 Florida case that appears in the research trail. Provide the name and citation of the case, and briefly explain why the court cited the case you located for Question 3, above.

V. Internet

Many cases are available on the Internet. Depending on the source you use to search, you may be able to search by date, citation, or party name. Some sites also permit word searches. One source for Internet case research is Google Scholar.

One concern courts have about enforcing constructive trusts between unmarried partners is that doing so is, in essence, to permit a claim for "palimony." To research whether Florida courts have addressed this concern, access Google Scholar. (Hint: You can access Google Scholar from the main Google search engine page or at scholar.google.com.)

Select the "Case law" button under the search box and check Florida state courts. Click the down arrow in the search box to go to "Advanced Scholar Search." From the search screen, enter the following terms in the search boxes:

with **all** of the words	palimony
with the **exact phrase**	constructive trust

Execute the search. Review the search results. Provide the name and citation of a 1995 case in which the court used the doctrine of constructive trust to award temporary support to a woman seeking an annulment of her marriage, and briefly explain what the court said about "palimony."

Exercise 4.3
Researching Cases on Your Own

Name: _____   Due Date: _____

Professor: _____   Section: _____

Goal

To locate cases to answer a legal question.

Instructions

1. After each question, you will find space to write your answer. This is for your convenience while you are working on the exercise. After you finish your research, submit your answers in typewritten form on a separate answer sheet. Do not retype the questions. Your answer sheet should contain only the answers to the questions.

2. If you spend more than 20 minutes researching the legal question, use the troubleshooting hints in the General Instructions for this Workbook. If you are still unable to find the answer, stop and seek assistance.

3. Do not forget to update your research even though the questions do not prompt you to do so.

4. Reshelve all books as soon as you finish using them.

Problem Set
(circle one)   A B C D E F G H I J K L M N O P Q R

THE ASSIGNMENT

Review the legal question below, and conduct state case law research in the jurisdiction specified in your problem set to determine the answer. (Hint: Make sure that you locate *state* cases—not *federal* cases—to answer the question.)

Unlike the questions in Exercises 4.1 and 4.2 that directed you to specific information, this exercise requires you to conduct and evaluate the results of your research independently. If your professor permits you to choose between print and electronic research for this exercise, you may want to conduct research both ways to compare your results.

Legal Question

Your client, Estelle Pierce, bought a painting from Chrystal's, a well-known auction house. She contacted Chrystal's because she wanted to collect authentic works of art by American painters. As Chrystal's knew, Ms. Pierce was not a sophisticated art collector; she told Chrystal's she was looking to its expertise to make sure she purchased only authentic works. Chrystal's offered to sell Ms. Pierce a painting by Edmund Charles Tarbell, a well-known American painter, and to provide documentation attesting to its authenticity. After buying the painting for $40,000, Ms. Pierce learned that the painting was a fake worth only a few hundred dollars.

Ms. Pierce wants to sue Chrystal's. So far, no evidence shows that Chrystal's committed fraud by knowingly misrepresenting the authenticity of the painting. You need to find out whether Chrystal's may be liable for the tort of negligent misrepresentation. Specifically, you need to find out the elements or requirements of a negligent misrepresentation claim.

Jurisdictions

Problem Set A (Kansas)	Problem Set J (Florida)
Problem Set B (Texas)	Problem Set K (Minnesota)
Problem Set C (Alabama)	Problem Set L (jurisdiction assigned by your professor)
Problem Set D (Oklahoma)	Problem Set M (Maryland)
Problem Set E (Ohio)	Problem Set N (Wisconsin)
Problem Set F (jurisdiction assigned by your professor)	Problem Set O (Pennsylvania)
Problem Set G (Arizona)	Problem Set P (Utah)
Problem Set H (South Carolina)	Problem Set Q (Missouri)
Problem Set I (Illinois)	Problem Set R (jurisdiction assigned by your professor)

I. Selecting a Digest, Database, or Research Source

Indicate which print digest or electronic research source you will use to conduct your research.

II. Conducting Research

Record all the steps in your research process.

III. Determining Which Case(s) Apply

Provide the name and citation of at least one case, but no more than three cases, defining the requirements of a negligent misrepresentation claim.

IV. Answering the Legal Question

Based on the results of your research, identify the elements or requirements of a negligent misrepresentation claim.

Chapter 5
RESEARCH WITH CITATORS

Exercise 5.1
Researching Cases with Citators

Name: _____   Due Date: _____

Professor: _____   Section: _____

Goals

1. To learn how to check case citations electronically using Shepard's in Lexis and KeyCite in Westlaw.

2. To learn how to interpret electronic citator entries.

3. To understand the differences between Shepard's in Lexis and KeyCite in Westlaw.

Instructions

1. After each question, you will find space to write your answer. This is for your convenience while you are working on the exercise. After you finish your research, submit your answers in typewritten form on a separate answer sheet. Do not retype the questions. Your answer sheet should contain only the answers to the questions.

2. If you spend more than 15 minutes trying to find the answer to any individual question, use the troubleshooting hints in the General Instructions for this Workbook. If you are still unable to find the answer, stop and seek assistance.

Problem Set
(circle one)   A   B   C   D   E

THE ASSIGNMENT

Once you have located one or more cases relevant to a legal question, the next step in the research process is using a citator, both to verify the continued validity of the cases you have found and to locate additional research references relevant to the legal question. This exercise guides you through the process of using two electronic citators: Shepard's in Lexis and KeyCite in Westlaw. Although you would ordinarily locate cases through other research tools before using a citator, this exercise provides the citations you will use.

I. Review Questions

A. Which one or more of the following statements is true about a case whose citator entry shows a red stop sign (Shepard's in Lexis) or a red flag (KeyCite in Westlaw): (a) the case is no longer valid and cannot be cited for any purpose; (b) the case is no longer valid for at least one of the points it discusses; (c) the case may be valid for one or more of the points it discusses.

B. If you locate a case whose citator entry shows a yellow triangle (Shepard's in Lexis) or a yellow flag (KeyCite in Westlaw), can you rely on that case as valid without further research? Explain your answer.

C. Both Shepard's in Lexis and KeyCite in Westlaw list the history of a citing case and citing sources that have cited the original case. What is the difference in the way the *citing cases* in these two services are organized? Explain your answer.

II. Using KeyCite and Shepard's

A client has come to you with the following legal question:

Your client is Amanda Pearson. She suffered serious injuries as a result of side effects of prescription medication she was taking. She says she was not warned of the possible side effects and would not have taken the medication if she had known about the dangers. Her doctor is a personal friend, and she does not wish to sue him. She wants to know if she can sue the drug manufacturer for failing to warn her about the medication's possible side effects. You know that a drug manufacturer is sometimes protected from liability to consumers if it provides adequate warnings to the prescribing physician under a doctrine known as the "learned-intermediary doctrine." You need to research the law of your jurisdiction to see whether it applies the learned-intermediary doctrine to protect drug manufacturers from liability for failure to warn consumers about the risks of prescription medications.

Assume that you located the case listed below for your problem set and need to find out whether it is still valid and whether it can lead you to additional cases relevant to the legal question. In the questions, the term "original case" refers to the case listed below and the term "citing sources" refers to sources citing the original case. Locate the original case for your problem set, and answer the questions below.

Original Case

Problem Set A	*Stone v. Smith, Kline & French Laboratories*, 447 So. 2d 1301 (Ala. 1984)
Problem Set B	*Strumph v. Schering Corp.*, 606 A.2d 1140 (N.J. Super. Ct. App. Div. 1992)
Problem Set C	*MacDonald v. Ortho Pharmaceuticals Corp.*, 475 N.E.2d 65 (Mass. 1985)
Problem Set D	*Wyeth Laboratories, Inc. v. Fortenberry*, 530 So. 2d 688 (Miss. 1988)
Problem Set E	*Terhune v. A.H. Robins Co.*, 577 P.2d 975 (Wash. 1978)

A. Checking Case Citations with KeyCite on Westlaw

Shepard's is not available in Westlaw. Westlaw has its own citator called KeyCite. Although KeyCite is similar to Shepard's, the two services are not identical. The questions below guide you through the process of using KeyCite in Westlaw.

1. Retrieve the original case for your problem set. Briefly explain why this case might be relevant to your research.

2. A status flag appears near the caption of the original case. Describe the notation, and explain what it signifies about the case.

3. View the information under the "Negative Treatment" tab.

   Is the original case valid for the proposition it states that is relevant to your research (i.e., whether the jurisdiction applies the learned-intermediary doctrine to drug manufacturers)? (Hint: You may need to review one or more of the cases in the KeyCite entry to answer this question.)

4. View the "Citing References." Notice that they are organized by cases, trial court orders, secondary sources, etc. It is important to pay attention to the type of document in the entry because some have no effect on the continued validity of the citing case (e.g., cases decided by courts outside the controlling jurisdiction or motions filed in related cases), while others may be critical to your understanding of the law in your jurisdiction. Click on "Cases" under the "View" menu on the left side of the screen. In the "Narrow" filters (also on the left side of the screen), open the state jurisdictions. (Hint: Under "Jurisdiction," click on "State.") How many of the cases are from the same state as the original case? (Hint: Look for cases from the state's courts, not cases from the federal courts from the state. The number of cases from each state is listed to the right of each state's name.)

5. KeyCite entries contain references to West headnotes. A headnote summarizes a point of law discussed in the original case. A headnote reference in a KeyCite entry identifies a proposition of law for which a citing source cites the original case. Thus, if a point of law discussed in the original case is summarized in headnote 1, and the KeyCite entry lists a citing case with a reference to headnote 1, you know that the citing case cited the original case for the proposition summarized in headnote 1 of the original case. Headnote references can help you identify authorities that cite the original case on specific issues.

   You can limit the KeyCite display to show only the information most relevant to your research. You want to display state cases from the same state as the original case and then show only cases that cite the original case for the proposition summarized in the headnote listed below for your problem set. To do so, be sure the "Citing References" tab is selected. Limit the view to cases. Using the menu options, select the checkbox for state cases from the same state as the original case. Specify the headnote topic and number listed below for your problem set. (Hint: You may need to use the "Specify" buttons to find your headnote topic.) Filter the results to display the limited entry.

Headnote Reference

Problem Set A	Headnote 2	(Products liability headnote on learned intermediary)
Problem Set B	Headnote 2	(Products liability headnote on learned intermediary)
Problem Set C	Headnote 3	(Products liability headnote on intermediaries and third parties, in general)
Problem Set D	Headnote 5	(Products liability headnote on learned intermediary)
Problem Set E	Headnote 2	(Products liability headnote on learned intermediary)

The display will be limited to those cases from the same state as the original case with the headnote reference for your problem set.

Click on the link to one of the cases to see what the citing source says about the original case.

Provide the name and citation of the case you selected, and briefly explain what the citing case says about the original case.

(Hints: You may find more than one case from the appropriate jurisdiction that discusses the headnote for your problem set. You can choose any case that discusses the appropriate headnote. It does not matter whether the case also discusses other headnotes.)

6. Clear the filters by clicking "Undo Filters." Under "View," select "Secondary Sources" and "ALR." Provide the citation (as it appears in KeyCite) of an ALR Annotation that cites the original case. (Hint: The entry may list more than one ALR Annotation. You only need to provide one citation to answer this question. Do not cite an annotation that has been superseded.)

B. Checking Case Citations in Shepard's

Shepard's is available electronically only in Lexis.

1. Shepardize the original case for your problem set. The citations are repeated below.

Original Case

Problem Set A	*Stone v. Smith, Kline & French Laboratories*, 447 So. 2d 1301 (Ala. 1984)
Problem Set B	*Strumph v. Schering Corp.*, 606 A.2d 1140 (N.J. Super. Ct. App. Div. 1992)
Problem Set C	*MacDonald v. Ortho Pharmaceuticals Corp.*, 475 N.E.2d 65 (Mass. 1985)
Problem Set D	*Wyeth Laboratories, Inc. v. Fortenberry*, 530 So. 2d 688 (Miss. 1988)
Problem Set E	*Terhune v. A.H. Robins Co.*, 577 P.2d 975 (Wash. 1978)

In the red search box, type "shep:" followed by the citation for the original case for your problem set (e.g., shep: 447 So. 2d 1301). Execute the search.

A Shepard's signal appears near the case name and citation. Describe the notation and explain what it signifies about the case.

2. Although Shepard's in Lexis and KeyCite in Westlaw provide largely the same information about cases, the two services are not identical. For example, the organization of the information in the two services differs.

Review the Citing Decisions in the Shepard's entry. Explain how the organization of the Citing Decisions in Shepard's differs from the organization of the Citing References in KeyCite.

3. Lexis adds headnotes to cases as research references just like West and many official state reporters do. Review the Citing Decisions and identify one or more cases from the same state as the original case with the LexisNexis Headnote reference below for your problem set. To do so, click "Citing Decisions," and in the "Narrow By" options in the left margin click on the headnote number for your problem set. Provide the name and citation of one case.

(Hints: Be sure to use the LexisNexis Headnote reference to answer this question. You may find more than one case that discusses the headnote for your problem set. You can choose any case that discusses the headnote. It does not matter whether the case also discusses other headnotes. Be sure to choose a case from the same state as the original case.)

LexisNexis Headnote Reference

Problem Set A	LexisNexis Headnote 2
Problem Set B	LexisNexis Headnote 2
Problem Set C	LexisNexis Headnote 2
Problem Set D	LexisNexis Headnote 4
Problem Set E	LexisNexis Headnote 2

4. If the original case has been cited in secondary sources such as treatises or law review articles, Shepard's will include those sources in the entry. Select "Other Citing Sources" and then narrow to "Law Reviews" or "Treatises" to locate the section corresponding to the document type indicated below for your problem set.

   Provide the citation (as it appears in the Shepard's entry) to the first document of the appropriate type for your problem set in the Shepard's entry.

Portion of Shepard's Entry

Problem Set A	Law Reviews
Problem Set B	Law Reviews
Problem Set C	Law Reviews
Problem Set D	Law Reviews
Problem Set E	Law Reviews

5. In addition to viewing the full entry, you can customize the display in Shepard's to identify sources that treat the original case in a specific way. Select "Citing Decisions." Use the "Narrow By" options in the left margin to limit the display as indicated for your problem set.

   Provide the name and citation of a Citing Decision that treats the original case in the manner indicated for your problem set.

   (Hint: You may find more than one case that treats the original case in the manner indicated for your problem set. You only need to list one case in answer to this question.)

Restricted Display Option

Problem Set A	Criticized
Problem Set B	Followed
Problem Set C	Criticized
Problem Set D	Distinguished
Problem Set E	Criticized

Exercise 5.2
Researching Statutes and Secondary Sources with Citators

Name: _____ Due Date: _____

Professor: _____ Section: _____

Goal

To understand Shepard's and KeyCite entries for statutes and secondary sources.

Instructions

1. After each question, you will find space to write your answer. This is for your convenience while you are working on the exercise. After you finish your research, submit your answers in typewritten form on a separate answer sheet. Do not retype the questions. Your answer sheet should contain only the answers to the questions.

2. If you spend more than 15 minutes trying to find the answer to any individual question, use the troubleshooting hints in the General Instructions for this Workbook. If you are still unable to find the answer, stop and seek assistance.

There are no separate problem sets for this exercise.

THE ASSIGNMENT

Exercise 5.1 shows you how to use Shepard's and KeyCite in conjunction with case research. This exercise illustrates Shepard's and KeyCite entries for other forms of primary and secondary authority.

I. Shepard's Citations on Lexis

A. Shepard's is available for federal and state statutes (as is KeyCite). Shepard's will provide current information about amendments and other legislative actions affecting the statute's status, as well as citations to cases and other sources citing the statute.

Retrieve the following federal statute in Lexis and answer the questions that follow:

18 USCS § 700

1. Briefly explain what the statute prohibits.

2. Shepardize the statute by clicking the "Shepardize this document" link in the right margin. What negative treatment has the statute received from the U.S. Supreme Court?

B. Shepard's is available for law review articles (as is KeyCite). If you find a law review article that supports your analysis, it would be good to know whether the article was persuasive to courts in your jurisdiction. A citator will tell you whether the article has been cited in other sources, including court opinions.

Shepardize the following citation:

81 U. Det. Mercy L. Rev. 267

Provide the name of a case from the Supreme Court of West Virginia that cites this article.

II. KeyCite on Westlaw

A. KeyCite is available for Restatements of the law (as is Shepard's). The citator entry for a Restatement provision can help you determine whether a particular jurisdiction follows the Restatement.

Locate the provision of the *Restatement (Third) of Torts* addressing "Liability of Commercial Seller Or Distributor For Harm Caused By Defective Prescription Drugs And Medical Devices" using the following citation (which takes you to the *Restatement (Third) of Torts: Products Liability* § 6):

rest 3d torts-pl s 6

View the Citing References. Provide the name of a case decided in 2000 by the United States Court of Appeals for the Second Circuit that cites this Restatement provision.

B. KeyCite is available for A.L.R. Annotations. Retrieve the following A.L.R. Annotation from its citation and answer the questions below:

57 alr5th 1

1. What is the title of the Annotation?

2. View the Citing References. Provide the name of a Nebraska case that cites the Annotation.

Exercise 5.3
Checking Case Citations on Your Own

Name: _____   Due Date: _____

Professor: _____   Section: _____

Goal

To update case research and locate research references using a citator.

Instructions

1. After each question, you will find space to write your answer. This is for your convenience while you are working on the exercise. After you finish your research, submit your answers in typewritten form on a separate answer sheet. Do not retype the questions. Your answer sheet should contain only the answers to the questions.

2. If you spend more than 20 minutes checking the case citation, use the troubleshooting hints in the General Instructions for this Workbook. If you are still unable to find the answers to the questions, stop and seek assistance.

Problem Set
(circle one)   A   B   C   D   E   F   G   H   I   J   K   L   M   N   O   P   Q   R

THE ASSIGNMENT

This exercise is related to Exercise 4.3, Researching Cases on Your Own. You will need to use the citation to one of the cases you located to answer the legal question for your problem set in Exercise 4.3 for this exercise. The legal question and problem set jurisdictions are repeated below. If you have not completed Exercise 4.3, your professor will provide you with a citation.

This exercise requires you to use a citator to check the validity of a case and locate research references relevant to an issue discussed in the case. For any citation you use to complete this exercise, you should be able to determine whether the case remains valid. Depending on the case, however, you may or may not find additional research references through the citator. You may find that the case has an extensive history and has been cited numerous times, or you may find that it has never been cited at all.

Legal Question

Your client, Estelle Pierce, bought a painting from Chrystal's, a well-known auction house. She contacted Chrystal's because she wanted to collect authentic works of art by American painters. As Chrystal's knew, Ms. Pierce was not a sophisticated art collector; she told Chrystal's she was looking to its expertise to make sure she purchased only authentic works. Chrystal's offered to sell Ms. Pierce a painting by Edmund Charles Tarbell, a well-known American painter, and to provide documentation attesting to its authenticity. After buying the painting for $40,000, Ms. Pierce learned that the painting was a fake worth only a few hundred dollars.

Ms. Pierce wants to sue Chrystal's. So far, no evidence shows that Chrystal's committed fraud by knowingly misrepresenting the authenticity of the painting. You need to find out whether Chrystal's may be liable for the tort of negligent misrepresentation. Specifically, you need to find out the elements or requirements of a negligent misrepresentation claim.

Jurisdictions

Problem Set A (Kansas)	Problem Set J (Florida)
Problem Set B (Texas)	Problem Set K (Minnesota)
Problem Set C (Alabama)	Problem Set L (jurisdiction assigned by your professor)
Problem Set D (Oklahoma)	Problem Set M (Maryland)
Problem Set E (Ohio)	Problem Set N (Wisconsin)
Problem Set F (jurisdiction assigned by your professor)	Problem Set O (Pennsylvania)
Problem Set G (Arizona)	Problem Set P (Utah)
Problem Set H (South Carolina)	Problem Set Q (Missouri)
Problem Set I (Illinois)	Problem Set R (jurisdiction assigned by your professor)

I. Locating the Case

Locate the case for your problem set, and review it. Briefly explain why it might be relevant to your research on the legal question. (Hint: The case citation does not appear in this exercise. You should use either one of the citations you located for Exercise 4.3, Researching Cases on Your Own, or a citation provided by your professor.)

II. Selecting a Citator

Indicate which citator(s) you will use to check the citation.

III. Using the Citator and Interpreting the Entry

Enter the citation in the citator(s) you have decided to use, and answer the questions below.

A. Determining the Validity of the Case

Is the case still authoritative in the jurisdiction where it was decided for the propositions of law that made it relevant to your research? Explain your answer. (Hint: You may not be able to answer this question solely from the citator entries. You may need to review some of the citing sources to answer this question.)

B. Locating Research References

Although the case you are checking states a rule that is relevant to the legal question, you need to find additional authority to support the rule. Review the citator entry to identify additional cases in your jurisdiction that state the rule you are researching. List up to three cases you could cite for additional support for the rule. If the entry does not list any cases that would provide additional support, answer "No relevant citing cases." An unpublished table disposition or a court order should not be cited. (Hint: Be sure to narrow the scope of the cases you review to only those state cases in your jurisdiction. If that number is large, narrowing by the phrase "negligent misrepresentation" or by the relevant headnote will reduce the number of cases to review.)

Chapter 6
STATUTORY RESEARCH

Exercise 6.1
Researching Statutes in Print

Name: _____ Due Date: _____

Professor: _____ Section: _____

Goals

1. To locate statutes in print using the subject index and popular name table.
2. To update print statutory research with pocket parts and cumulative or noncumulative supplements.
3. To locate research references using statutory annotations.

Instructions

1. After each question, you will find space to write your answer. This is for your convenience while you are working on the exercise. After you finish your research, submit your answers in typewritten form on a separate answer sheet. Do not retype the questions. Your answer sheet should contain only the answers to the questions.

2. If you spend more than 15 minutes trying to find the answer to any individual question, use the troubleshooting hints in the General Instructions for this Workbook. If you are still unable to find the answer, stop and seek assistance.

3. Although some questions include hints reminding you to update your research, others do not. Do not forget to update your research in all sources even if the question does not prompt you to do so.

4. Reshelve all books as soon as you finish using them.

Problem Set
(circle one)   A   B   C   D   E   F   G   H   I   J   K   L   M   N   O

THE ASSIGNMENT

You need to answer several legal questions by conducting statutory research. This exercise will guide you through the process of researching statutes in print. As you conduct your research, you will need to provide answers to the legal questions. Answer the legal questions for this exercise using only the text of the statutes you locate; do not conduct additional research.

I. Review Questions

A. How do federal public laws, session laws, and codified statutes differ?

B. If you had a choice between using U.S.C. and U.S.C.S. to research federal law, which would you use? Be sure to explain your answer.

C. Explain the difference between an official code and an unofficial code.

II. State Statutory Research

Locate the state code for your problem set to answer the questions below.

State Code

Problem Set A	Arizona Revised Statutes Annotated
Problem Set B	West's Annotated California Codes
Problem Set C	West's Colorado Revised Statutes Annotated
Problem Set D	Connecticut General Statutes Annotated
Problem Set E	West's Florida Statutes Annotated
Problem Set F	West's Smith-Hurd Illinois Compiled Statutes Annotated
Problem Set G	Burns Indiana Statutes Annotated

Problem Set H	*Iowa Code Annotated*
Problem Set I	*West's Annotated Code of Maryland* or *Michie's Annotated Code of Maryland*
Problem Set J	*Vernon's Annotated Missouri Statutes*
Problem Set K	*McKinney's Consolidated New York Laws Annotated*
Problem Set L	*Purdon's Pennsylvania Consolidated Statutes Annotated*
Problem Set M	*Code of Virginia 1950*
Problem Set N	*West's Revised Code of Washington Annotated*
Problem Set O	*Jurisdiction assigned by your professor*

A note about state codes: For Problem Sets A through N, this exercise directs you to use a specific version of a state's code. A state's code may be published by more than one publisher. If you use a version of the state code different from the one specified above, you should be able to locate the correct statutory provisions, but the index entries and information in the annotations may differ between the two versions of the code.

A. Often the answer to a question involving statutory research will not be found in a single section of the code. Instead, statutory research ordinarily requires you to research the complete statutory scheme, which may encompass multiple sections of the code. Many statutory schemes include a definitions section defining key terms, which can help you determine whether the scheme applies to the issue you are researching. To answer the state statutory research question in this exercise, you will need to locate the definitions section of a statutory scheme.

Here is your research situation:

You are general counsel for a major medical center and are responsible for ensuring that the center's policies and procedures comply with state law. The medical center wants to expand its services to include removing and transplanting human tendons through its orthopedic center. A tendon is not an organ; it is classified as human tissue. You know that state law regarding anatomical gifts applies to donations of body parts such as organs. You need to find out whether human tendons constitute body parts under the anatomical gift law.

1. Locate the general index for the state code. The index will refer you to relevant statutory provisions on the subject you are researching. For your research situation, look up the following search terms:

   Anatomical Gifts
   Definitions
   OR
   Anatomical Gifts
   Generally

(Hint for Problem Set L: The index entry for Anatomical Gifts refers you to the entry for "Gifts." Look up the term "Gifts," and then locate the subheading for "Anatomical Gifts.")

The index may refer you to a specific section containing definitions, or it may refer you to a range of sections. The designation "et seq." refers to sections following the one listed in the index entry. If the index refers you to multiple sections, you will need to review the referenced sections to locate the definitions section.

(Hint for Problem Set O: You may need to review different or additional subject entries in the index to find the information you need.)

Turn to the section(s) listed in the index, and locate the section containing definitions. Be sure to check the pocket part and soft cover supplement, if any. If the section has been enacted recently, it may not appear in the main volume of the code and may appear only in the pocket part or soft cover supplement.

Provide the subject name, if appropriate, and section number for the section containing definitions. (Hint: Some state codes are organized by subject names, e.g., "Education § 100." If the code for your problem set is organized by subject, provide the subject name along with the section number for the section containing definitions. If not, provide only the section number.)

2. Define the term "body part," "part," or "body." Be sure to check the pocket part and soft cover supplement, if any, to update your research. (Hint: The precise term that appears in the definitions section will vary depending on which problem set you complete.)

3. Review the annotations to the definitions section. The annotations list sources that have cited or discussed the code section, as well as other research references. Provide the information requested about the source listed for your problem set.

(Hints: If the statute appears in the main volume, be sure to check the pocket part or soft cover supplement for updated annotations. If the statute appears in both the main volume and pocket part, the annotation source could be in either place.)

Annotation Information

Problem Set A	The name and citation of a 2007 law review article
Problem Set B	The name and citation of a 1993 law review article
Problem Set C	The subject name and section numbers of an encyclopedia entry in Am. Jur. 2d.

Problem Set D	The name and citation of a 1991 law review article
Problem Set E	The name and citation of a 1970 law review article by Luis Kutner
Problem Set F	The name and citation of a 1983 case
Problem Set G	The name and citation of a 1989 law review article
Problem Set H	The name and citation of a 2008 law review article
Problem Set I	The language inserted in, or added to, subsection (d) by amendment in 2008
Problem Set J	The name and citation of a 1996 law review article
Problem Set K	The name and citation of a 1975 case
Problem Set L	The name and citation of a 2003 law review article
Problem Set M	The name and citation of a 2000 or 2007 law review article
Problem Set N	The name and citation of a 2008 case
Problem Set O	The name of a source listed in the annotations. If no sources are listed, answer "none" for this question.

4. Based on the information you found, does human tissue constitute a body part under state law governing anatomical gifts? Be sure to explain your answer.

B. As noted above, statutory research ordinarily requires you to research a complete statutory scheme. You will need to locate an additional section of the statute you located for Question A, above, to complete your research into the following matter:

In addition to determining the applicability of state anatomical gifts laws to tendon transplant procedures, you also need to evaluate the medical center's procedures for organ donations. The existing policy places no restrictions on which physicians may participate in an organ donation procedure. You are concerned that this policy may need to be revised to comply with state law.

Often, a code will provide an outline of the sections in a particular chapter or title. A good way to find related code provisions (including the provision you need to answer the questions below) is to use the statutory outline that appears at or near the beginning of the article, subchapter, chapter, or title of the code. (Hint: Usually the outline appears in the main volume of the code. If the statute has recently been enacted or substantially modified, you may find a full or partial outline in the pocket part or soft cover supplement.)

1. Locate the section of the act addressing which physicians may participate in an organ donation procedure. This information appears in a provision that relates to procurement organizations,

and more specifically, addresses rights and/or duties of an organ procurement organization upon the donor's death.

(Hint for Problem Set N: Locate the section concerning physical removal of donated body parts.)

Provide the section number. Which physicians, if any, are prohibited from participating in procedures to remove or transplant a donated organ?

2. Based on what you found, does the medical center need to revise its policy? If not, why not? If so, how does the policy need to be changed?

III. Federal Statutory Research

The process of federal statutory research is similar to the process for state statutory research. To answer the questions below, locate either *United States Code Annotated* (U.S.C.A.) or *United States Code Service* (U.S.C.S.).

You can research the federal code using a subject index. The subject index will refer you to titles and sections within the federal code that pertain to the subject you are researching. Sometimes Congress names an act. These acts, such as the USA Patriot Act, are known by their popular names. If you know the popular name of an act, you can find its citation in the Popular Name Table in U.S.C.A. or the Table of Statutes by Popular Name in U.S.C.S. These tables list statutes alphabetically by name and will direct you to the title(s) and section(s) where the act is codified.

For this part of the exercise, you are continuing your research into matters affecting the medical center. You need to research the federal code to answer the questions for your problem set. Using *either* the subject index *or* the popular name table for *either* U.S.C.A. *or* U.S.C.S., locate statutory provisions that answer the federal statutory question for your problem set.

Federal Statutory Question

Problem Set A, B, C, D, & E	You are continuing your review of the medical center's policies and procedures. The medical center offers ophthalmic services and operates its own optometry. The individuals who work in the optometry are licensed by the state to prescribe corrective lenses and dispense glasses and contact lenses. You need to find out whether the optometry is subject to the Fairness to Contact Lens Consumers Act. Specifically: (1) Are the individuals who dispense contact lenses through the optometry considered contact lens "prescribers"? (2) Under what circumstances are contact lens "prescribers" required to provide a patient with a written copy of the patient's contact lens prescription?

Problem Set F, G, H, I, & J	The medical center treats patients from across the country, and many patients must travel long distances for treatment. The medical center runs a nonprofit foundation that provides housing for patients' family members if those family members live a long distance from the medical center. The foundation wants to begin a fundraising campaign by placing calls to people across the U.S. to solicit funds for the family housing program. You need to find out whether this fundraising effort is subject to the Telemarketing and Consumer Fraud and Abuse Prevention Act. Specifically: (1) Would a telephone campaign seeking charitable contributions from people across the country constitute "telemarketing"? (2) If the foundation were to violate federal telemarketing rules, how long would a private person have to bring a civil action against the foundation?
Problem Set K, L, M, N, & O	The medical center treats many children. It operates a Web site for children facing serious illnesses. The Web site collects personal information from children and therefore is subject to federal law governing children's online privacy. You need to review the policies and procedures for operation of the Web site to make sure they comply with the Children's Online Privacy Protection Act of 1998. Specifically: (1) Does the law governing online privacy apply to a "child" over age 12? (2) Can the medical center, as the operator of the Web site, be held liable under state or federal law for disclosing a child's personal information to the child's parent?

A. Indicate how you located the relevant act.

B. The act spans multiple sections of the code. Provide the number of the title where the statute is codified, and provide the section numbers for the first and last sections of the statute.

C. Review the chapter outline, and locate the provisions that answer the federal statutory questions for your problem set.
   1. Briefly answer the first question. Provide the section number of the section where you found the answer. Be sure to explain your answer.

2. Briefly answer the second question. Provide the section number of the section where you found the answer. Be sure to explain your answer.

Exercise 6.2
Researching Statutes Electronically

Name: _____   Due Date: _____

Professor: _____   Section: _____

Goals

1. To locate statutes electronically by using an electronic index, browsing a table of contents, searching by popular name, and executing a word search.
2. To update statutory research and locate research references using electronic statutory citators.

Instructions

1. After each question, you will find space to write your answer. This is for your convenience while you are working on the exercise. After you finish your research, submit your answers in typewritten form on a separate answer sheet. Do not retype the questions. Your answer sheet should contain only the answers to the questions.

2. If you spend more than 15 minutes trying to find the answer to any individual question, use the troubleshooting hints in the General Instructions for this Workbook. If you are still unable to find the answer, stop and seek assistance.

There are no separate problem sets for this exercise.

THE ASSIGNMENT

In Exercise 6.1, you answered legal questions by conducting statutory research in print. To answer the legal questions in this exercise, you will need to conduct additional statutory research using electronic resources. Answer the questions using only the text of the statutes you locate; do not conduct additional research.

You can locate statutes electronically in a variety of ways. Three common search techniques are: (1) retrieving a statute from its citation; (2) searching by subject using a statutory index or by browsing the table of contents of a code; and (3) executing a word search. Exercise 1.2, Introduction to Electronic Research, illustrates how to retrieve a statute from its citation. This exercise illustrates the subject and word searching options. You can also update statutory research and locate research references by using KeyCite in Westlaw or Shepard's in Lexis. You will use both updating services in the questions for this exercise.

I. WestlawNext

Begin your research by using Westlaw to locate authority relevant to the following research situation:

You are general counsel for a major medical center that is located in New Jersey. The medical center is a nonprofit entity (as defined under state and federal law) and relies on many volunteers to assist in providing comfort and assistance to patients and their families. Volunteers receive no compensation for their work and are not required to be licensed for the ministerial tasks they perform. Volunteers are instructed never to try to diagnose any ailment or provide any medication to any patient and to call for a member of the medical staff if any patient needs medical help.

Mark Sandofsky was a volunteer at the medical center. He is trained as an actuary; he has no medical training of any kind. Mr. Sandofsky was assisting a patient, Alma DeSantis, when Ms. DeSantis complained of a headache. Instead of calling for a member of the medical staff, Mr. Sandofsky provided Ms. DeSantis with an over-the-counter headache medication that he carried for his personal use. Unfortunately, Ms. DeSantis suffered serious complications from taking the over-the-counter medication because it was incompatible with several prescription medications she was taking. Ms. DeSantis is now suing the medical center for negligence and Mr. Sandofsky for gross negligence. You need to find out whether federal law protects the medical center or Mr. Sandofsky from liability for Ms. DeSantis's claims.

A. Searching by Subject in WestlawNext

One way to locate statutes is by searching by subject. WestlawNext provides electronic access to the statutory index to many codes. Most electronic research services do not provide indices, but when one is available, it is an excellent way to search for statutes by subject. Browsing a code's table of contents is another way to search by subject and to make sure you locate all relevant provisions within a statute.

To determine whether federal law protects the medical center or a volunteer from negligence claims, begin by accessing the index to *United States Code Annotated*, the version of the federal code available in WestlawNext. From the home page, choose the option to search United States Code Annotated (USCA). You can do this by following the link to "Statutes & Court Rules" under the "All Content" tab or by clicking on the "Federal Materials" tab. Once you access USCA, look for the list of "Tools & Resources." Click on the link to "USCA Index" in the "Tools & Resources" list.

Once you have accessed the USCA statutes index, you will see an alphabetical list of index topics. Locate the index entry for "Volunteers" and subtopic "Protection." (Hint: Open the entry for Volunteers to see the subtopics listed under it.)

The index refers you to a section, followed by the notation "et seq." This means that the section referenced and following sections may be relevant to your research. Click on the link to the section referenced to view the section, and answer the questions below.

1. This is the first section of an act with multiple sections. Review the section you retrieved and the Historical and Statutory Notes in the accompanying annotations. What is the name of the section, and what is the short title of the act of which it is a part?

   (Hint: The short title appears under the History tab in the Editor's and Revisor's Notes.)

2. Go back to the Document tab for this section. This section does not answer your research question. To view an outline of the rest of the sections in the act, click on the "Table of Contents" link. Provide the first and last section numbers of the act as listed in the table of contents.

3. Review the sections of the act, and answer the questions that follow:
   a. Is Mr. Sandofsky a "volunteer" under the act? Provide the number of the section you used to answer this question. Be sure to explain your answer.

   b. Is Mr. Sandofsky protected from liability for gross negligence under the act? Provide the number of the section you used to answer this question. Be sure to explain your answer.

   c. Is the medical center protected from liability for negligence under the act? Provide the number of the section you used to answer this question. Be sure to explain your answer.

B. Updating Statutory Research with KeyCite

Once you retrieve a section of a statute, you can use KeyCite to check it. The KeyCite entry will contain information on the history or status of the section, as well as the most complete listing of sources that have cited the section.

Go to the third section of the act you retrieved for Question A1 (42 U.S.C.A. § 14503), and answer the questions below.

1. Review the annotations accompanying the statute. Are any cases summarized in the annotations? If so, how many? (Hint: In WestlawNext, use the Notes of Decisions tab.)

2. Although the Notes of Decisions can contain summaries of many cases that cite a statute, not all are listed there. A citator will list all citing cases. To view cases citing the section, click on the "Citing References" link. How many citing cases appear in the KeyCite entry?

C. Word Searching

In WestlawNext, you can conduct a word search with or without selecting a database for your search. Because your search will retrieve many types of authority (statutes, cases, secondary sources, etc.), you can retrieve multiple forms of authority in a single search. If you are not sure what type of authority will help you answer a research question, or when you know you need multiple types of authority, a global search can be effective. But having all results in a single search may make it difficult to focus on the most relevant or most authoritative sources. You must evaluate the results carefully to make sure you locate and use the best authority available to resolve your research issue.

Continue your research into Ms. DeSantis's claims by using a word search to determine whether state law applies to your research situation. Specifically, you need to determine whether state charitable immunity law protects the medical center from liability for Ms. DeSantis's claim.

Locate the global search box. Use the jurisdiction selection box next to the search box to limit the jurisdiction to New Jersey. (Hint: Check the box for New Jersey and uncheck all other boxes.)

Enter the following search in the global search box, and execute the search:

charitable immunity

Review the search results. Notice that it retrieves thousands of documents organized by document type. Review the statutory results, and locate a statute that provides immunity from liability for negligence to nonprofit entities such as hospitals.

1. Provide the number of the section and the name of the annotated code.

2. Briefly describe what the section provides.

3. To claim charitable immunity, the medical center must qualify as a charitable institution. You need to find out whether this is a question for the court, or for the jury. The statutory language of the section you located for Questions 1 and 2, above, does not answer this question. Therefore, you must look for case law applying the statute to see if this question has been addressed.

    Review the Notes of Decisions accompanying the section. Is the determination of an entity's charitable status a question for the court or the jury? Provide the name and citation of a case that supports your answer. (Hint: The case summaries are organized by subject. Look for a subject heading that pertains to questions of law, or for the court. Click on the subject heading to go directly to case summaries under that heading.)

II. Lexis Advance

In this part of the exercise, you will continue your research by using Lexis Advance to research Florida state statutes to answer the following research question:

A patient received an organ transplant at a branch of the medical center located in Florida. The patient required a blood transfusion during the procedure. Although the transplant was successful, the patient developed a rare form of hepatitis from the blood transfusion and is seriously ill. Instead of bringing a tort claim, the patient has filed a breach of contract claim against the medical center. The patient alleges that the provision of blood constituted a contract for the sale of goods and that the medical center's use of tainted blood violated an implied warranty in the contract. You need to research Florida state law to determine whether any statutory provisions address the exclusion or modification of implied warranties to blood provided for transfusions.

A. Word Searching

For this part of the exercise, you need to research Florida state statutes. Use the Filters menus in the red search box to limit the Jurisdiction to Florida and the Category to Statutes and Legislation.

Enter the search below:

blood and implied warranty

1. Review the search results. Provide the section number of the statutory code that seems most applicable to your research situation.

2. Retrieve the section you listed in your answer to Question 1, above. Briefly summarize the relevant language from the statute.

3. Review the annotations accompanying the section. Scroll down until you find LexisNexis Notes and Case Notes. What must the plaintiff allege to maintain an action for breach of an implied warranty based on transfusion of tainted blood? Provide the name and citation of a case that supports your answer. (Hint: The case summaries are organized by subject. Look for a subject heading that pertains to blood and organ donations. Click on the arrow next to the subject heading to go directly to case summaries under that heading.)

4. The section you viewed is one section in a chapter comprised of multiple sections. Access the code's table of contents on the left side of the screen to see an outline of sections in the chapter. Browse the table of contents to locate two additional sections in this chapter of the code, one that addresses the implied warranty of merchantability and one that addresses the implied warranty of fitness for a particular purpose. Provide the numbers of the sections in the annotated code.

B. Shepardizing Statutes

You can check a statutory citation with Shepard's to locate information about the status of the statute and citations to sources that have cited the statute. Return to the statute you found for Question A1, above. Click on the "*Shepardize* this document" link in the right margin.

Review the Shepard's entry, and provide the name and citation of a case decided by the Florida Supreme Court that cites the statute.

III. Statutory Research on the Internet

The federal code and most state codes are available in unannotated form on the Internet. Depending on the source you use, you may be able to browse the code's table of contents, execute a key word search, or search for acts by popular name.

For this exercise, you are continuing your research into organ donation in your role as general counsel for a major medical center and must research the following situation:

> The medical center's doctors have a patient (Patient A) who needs a kidney transplant. The patient's cousin (Donor A) is willing to donate a kidney but is not a biological match. The doctors' colleagues at a New York hospital have another patient (Patient B) who also needs a kidney transplant. Patient B's spouse (Donor B) is willing to donate a kidney but is not a biological match. As luck would have it, however, Donor B is a biological match to Patient A and could donate a kidney to Patient A, while Donor A is a biological match to Patient B and could donate a kidney to Patient B. The donors are willing to donate to their biological matches so that both patients can receive the transplants they need. The doctors know, however, that it is illegal to sell or trade organs for compensation, and they are not sure whether this proposed arrangement is legal. You need to locate state and federal law regarding organ sales to see whether this type of paired donation is permissible.

A. State Statutory Research

For purposes of this exercise, assume that the procedures, if they are legal, would take place at the New York hospital, so you need to research New York law. You can locate New York statutes on the Internet in a variety of ways. One way is through Cornell Law School's Legal Information Institute Web site:

www.law.cornell.edu

From the home page, follow the links for "State law resources" and "Listing by jurisdiction." In the list of states, click on the link for New York, and choose the statutory option to search "New York Statutes," which takes you to the New York State Assembly site. Using the drop-down menu at the top of the page, select "Laws," and select "Laws of New York." This will bring up a search screen. You can execute a word search in the box above the listing of subjects covered in the consolidated laws. Execute the following search:

organ transplant

1. Provide the subject name and title number of the section that prohibits the sale of human organs.

2. Review the section. Does it specifically authorize or prohibit the type of paired donation the medical center's doctors want to perform? Be sure to explain your answer.

B. Federal Statutory Research

Having reviewed state law, you now need to research federal law to see if it permits paired organ donation. To research this issue, access the U.S. House of Representatives' web site containing the United States Code:

http://uscode.house.gov

Choose the option to search the U.S. Code, and enter the following terms in the box for Search Word(s):

organ and paired and donation

1. Review the search results. Provide the title and section number of the U.S.C. that is most relevant to your research.

2. Is the type of paired donation the center's doctors would like to perform permissible under the statute? Be sure to explain your answer.

3. After the text of the statute, you will find historical notes about the statute, including notes about some amendments to the statute. Congress has amended the statute. How was the statute amended in 2007?

Exercise 6.3
Researching Statutes on Your Own

Name: _____   Due Date: _____

Professor: _____   Section: _____

Goals

1. To locate statutes to answer a legal question.
2. To update statutory research.

Instructions

1. After each question, you will find space to write your answer. This is for your convenience while you are working on the exercise. After you finish your research, submit your answers in typewritten form on a separate answer sheet. Do not retype the questions. Your answer sheet should contain only the answers to the questions.

2. If you spend more than 20 minutes researching the legal question, use the troubleshooting hints in the General Instructions for this Workbook. If you are still unable to find the answer, stop and seek assistance.

3. Do not forget to update your research even though the questions do not prompt you to do so.

4. If you conduct research in print, reshelve all books as soon as you finish using them.

Problem Set
(circle one)   A B C D E F G H I J K L M N O

THE ASSIGNMENT

The medical center for which you conducted statutory research in Exercises 6.1 and 6.2 has come back to you with additional legal questions, set out below. Using the code for the jurisdiction for your problem set, conduct statutory research to determine the answers to the questions. The facts provided with the questions should lead you to a statutory scheme relevant to the questions. Unless your professor instructs you differently, answer the questions using only the text of the code section(s) you locate; do not conduct additional research.

If your professor permits you to choose between print and electronic research for this exercise, you may want to conduct research both ways to compare your results.

Here is the research situation:

The medical center has established an alternative healing center at which patients can receive nontraditional treatment, including massage and acupuncture. The director of the center wants to hire a therapist to conduct training sessions for the center's therapists and possibly treat patients. The therapist is only licensed in a neighboring state. The neighboring state has licensure requirements identical to those in the state where the medical center is located. The therapist has never faced any disciplinary action in the licensing state.

Problem Set	Jurisdiction	Legal Question
A	Arizona	The therapist is a massage practitioner and wishes to obtain a license in Arizona. What provision for a reciprocal license does state law make for a practitioner who already holds a license from another state?
B	California	The therapist is an acupuncture practitioner who will provide acupuncture demonstrations as part of an approved professional education program. For how long may an unlicensed guest acupuncturist provide acupuncture demonstrations without obtaining a license to practice in California?
C	Colorado	The therapist is an acupuncture practitioner and wishes to obtain a license in Colorado. What provision does state law make for licensing a practitioner who already holds a license from another state?
D	Connecticut	The therapist is a massage practitioner and wishes to obtain a license in Connecticut. What provision does state law make for licensing a practitioner who already holds a license from another state?
E	Florida	The therapist is an acupuncture practitioner and wishes to obtain a license in Florida. What provision does state law make for licensing a practitioner who already holds a license from another state?
F	Illinois	The therapist is a massage practitioner who will perform massage as part of an educational program. For how long may she do this while remaining exempt from state licensing requirements?
G	Indiana	The therapist is a massage practitioner and wishes to obtain a license (certification) in Indiana. Under what conditions can the practitioner obtain an Indiana license by endorsement of the license the practitioner already holds from another state?

H	Iowa	The therapist is an acupuncture practitioner. She treats patients using a range of therapies. She must obtain a license to provide any form of treatment that constitutes "acupuncture." What forms of treatment other than insertion of acupuncture needles, including adjunctive therapies, constitute the practice of acupuncture?
I	Maryland	The therapist is a massage practitioner and wishes to obtain a license in Maryland. What provision does state law make for licensing a practitioner who already holds a license from another state?
J	Missouri	The therapist is an acupuncture practitioner and wishes to obtain a license in Missouri. What provision does state law make for licensing a practitioner who already holds a license from another state?
K	New York	The therapist is an acupuncture practitioner. She will provide acupuncture training in a formal course of study registered in the state. Under what circumstances is the practitioner exempt from state licensing requirements in connection with providing acupuncture training as a faculty member?
L	Pennsylvania	The therapist is a massage practitioner and wishes to obtain a license in Pennsylvania. What provision does state law make for licensing a practitioner who already holds a license from another state?
M	Virginia	The therapist is a massage practitioner and wishes to obtain a license in Virginia. What qualifications does state law require for licensing a practitioner who already holds a license from another state?
N	Washington	The therapist is a massage practitioner and wishes to obtain a license in Washington. What provision does state law make for licensing a practitioner who already holds a license from another state?
O	Jurisdiction assigned by your professor	Define the practices of acupuncture and massage therapy under state law, using the definitions provided in the relevant licensing statutes. Answer any additional research question(s) assigned by your professor.

I. Conducting Research

Record all the steps in your research process.

II. Determining Which Statute Applies

List the statutory provision(s) you located.

III. Answering the Legal Question

Answer the legal question using the code section(s) you located. Be sure to explain your answer.

(Hint for Problem Set O: You may need to conduct additional research to answer all of the questions your professor has assigned for this exercise.)

Chapter 7
FEDERAL LEGISLATIVE HISTORY RESEARCH

Exercise 7.1
Researching the Legislative History of a Federal Statute Using Statutory Annotations

Name: _____   Due Date: _____

Professor: _____   Section: _____

Goal

To locate documents in the legislative history of a specific federal statute by statutory annotation in Westlaw.

Instructions

1. After each question, you will find space to write your answer. This is for your convenience while you are working on the exercise. After you finish your research, you must submit your answers in typewritten form. Do not retype the questions. The answer sheet should contain only the answers to the questions.

2. If you spend more than 15 minutes trying to find the answer to any individual question, use the troubleshooting hints in the General Instructions for this Workbook. If you are still unable to find the answer, stop and seek assistance.

Problem Set
(circle one)   A B C D E

THE ASSIGNMENT

You can research federal legislative history in two ways: You can search for the history of a specific statute, or you can search legislative history by subject. This exercise covers research into the legislative history of a specific statute, which is the way lawyers most frequently conduct legislative history research. Exercise 7.2 covers research into legislative history by subject.

For this exercise, you need to conduct research on legislative history related to your Client Matter, below. Although secondary sources, related statutes, and cases interpreting the statute can help you understand the statute, you have decided that you need to research the statute's legislative history to understand fully how the statute applies to your client's situation.

While you can conduct legislative history research in print, this exercise requires you to use only electronic sources, specifically WestlawNext.

I. Review Questions

A. List four sources of federal legislative history.

B. Rank the four sources you listed for Question A, above, in order from most authoritative to least authoritative, with source number 1 being the most authoritative and source number 4 being the least authoritative.

C. Briefly explain why the source you ranked first in Question B, above, is considered the most authoritative source of legislative history.

II. Using Statutory Annotations to Research the Legislative History of a Specific Statute

To research the legislative history of a specific federal statute, you first need to locate the statute and review the legislative information provided with the statute. U.S.C.A. annotations in WestlawNext contain references to the statute's Public Law (Pub. L.) number and its *United States Statutes at Large* (Stat.) citation, which are useful in researching legislative history. The annotation's "History" tab includes selected committee reports, Congressional Record entries, and other documents concerning the legislation. Annotations in Lexis Advance include references to the Public Law number and *United States Statutes at Large*, but not to committee reports.

Review the Client Matter. Use the search box in WestlawNext to retrieve the provision in U.S.C.A. for your problem set.

Client Matter and Statutory Provision

Problem Set A	You represent a consumer advocacy organization. You are concerned about mortgage companies who improperly charge homeowners for private mortgage insurance (or "PMI"). You want to research any federal remedies available to homeowners who have been improperly charged for PMI, and the legislative history of any such remedies.	12 U.S.C.A. § 4907
Problem Set B	You work for an organization of lobbyists who are concerned about federal lobbying rules and restrictions. You want to research federal statutes that govern congressional lobbyists and the accompanying legislative history.	2 U.S.C.A. § 1603
Problem Set C	You work for a child advocacy organization. You are interested in federal law and grant programs related to child welfare and the promotion of safe and stable families, as well as the legislative history of statutes establishing such programs.	42 U.S.C.A. § 629
Problem Set D	You work for an organization that advocates for the rights of persons with disabilities. You know that many disabled persons could find work if they had access to assistive technologies. Thus you are interested in any federal programs that support state efforts to provide disabled persons with assistive technology and the legislative history of such programs.	29 U.S.C.A. § 3001
Problem Set E	You work for an organization that advocates for good governance in Native American territories. You seek information on federal programs that provide funding and other assistance for expanded tribal justice systems and any legislative history on such programs.	25 U.S.C.A. § 3611

A. Briefly describe what the section provides.

B. The Public Law number and *United States Statutes at Large* citation for the section as originally enacted and for any subsequent amendments appear in parentheses immediately after the text of the statute and before the annotations.

Review the parenthetical following the text of the section you located for Question A, above, to answer the following questions.

1. Provide the Public Law number and *United States Statutes at Large* citation for the section as it was originally passed (not for any subsequent amendments).

    (Hint: Look for the earliest Public Law number and *United States Statutes at Large* citation.)

    (Hint for Problem Set C: Look for the Public Law number for the statute "as added.")

2. Click on the Public Law number link of the original Public Law to bring up the text of the original Act. (Hint: Click on the Public Law number link with the earliest date.) What is the name of the Act?

3. Now go back to the statute. Has the statute been amended by later acts of Congress? If so, how many times has it been amended?

C. Access the committee report for your problem set. Locate the link to the committee report under the "History" tab. The report you need may appear in the "Legislative History Materials" section, the "Editor's and Revisor's Notes" section, or both.

Click on the link to the report, and answer the following questions.

Committee Report Citation

Problem Set A	Senate Report No. 105-129, relating to the 1998 Acts
Problem Set B	House Report No. 104-339, relating to the 1995 Acts
Problem Set C	House Report No. 107-281, relating to the 2002 Acts
Problem Set D	House Report No. 108-514, relating to the 2004 Acts
Problem Set E	House Report No. 103-205, relating to the 1993 Acts

1. Provide the name of the committee that issued the report you located.

2. Before the statute was passed into law, it was assigned bill numbers in both the House of Representatives and the Senate. Provide the bill number for the version of the bill considered by the congressional committee that issued the report you located. (Hint: Look for the "S" number for bills considered by a Senate committee, and look for the "H.R." number for bills considered by a House committee.)

3. Provide the date of the Act's consideration in the Senate. If more than one date is listed, provide the latest date. (Hint: Be sure to provide the latest date, not the earliest (first) date.)

4. Skim the document, and answer the committee report question for your problem set below. (Hint: Go past the full text of the bill if it is reproduced at the beginning of the report to answer the question.)

Committee Report Question

Problem Set A	According to the section-by-section analysis of the bill, in the section on civil liability, what was one of the most controversial provisions of the bill, what happened to that provision, and why?
Problem Set B	How does the bill rectify inconsistencies and loopholes of current law?
Problem Set C	The primary improvements made to the PSSF program include adding two activities to the list of allowable activities. What are they? (Hint: Scroll down past the text of the bill to "I. Introduction, A. Purpose and Scope.")
Problem Set D	Briefly, what three principles of reform is the Assistive Technology Act of 2004 centered on? (Hint: Scroll down past the text of the bill, to the section on "Summary." List the principles only, not the accompanying explanations.)
Problem Set E	What has been the longstanding position of the Committee with regard to Indian tribes' rights? (Hint: Scroll down past the text of the bill, to the section on "Background and Need.")

Exercise 7.2
Researching the Legislative History of a Federal Statute by Subject

Name: _____ Due Date: _____

Professor: _____ Section: _____

Goal

To locate legislative history documents by subject in Lexis Advance and in a subscription research service.

Instructions

1. After each question, you will find space to write your answer. This is for your convenience while you are working on the exercise. After you finish your research, you must submit your answers in typewritten form. Do not retype the questions. The answer sheet should contain only the answers to the questions.

2. If you spend more than 15 minutes trying to find the answer to any individual question, use the troubleshooting hints in the General Instructions for this Workbook. If you are still unable to find the answer, stop and seek assistance.

Problem Set
(circle one)   A   B   C   D   E

THE ASSIGNMENT

In addition to locating legislative history through statutory annotations, as in Exercise 7.1, you can also locate legislative history by subject using a word search. This exercise requires you to use Lexis Advance to search the *Congressional Record* for floor debates and a subscription service, ProQuest Congressional, for committee testimony. Although this exercise requires you to use these specific services, you can also use WestlawNext or government resources such as Congress.gov to locate floor debates in the *Congressional Record*.

I. Locating Legislative History in the Congressional Record

This section requires you to locate a floor debate in the *Congressional Record* using Lexis Advance.

In order to locate the *Congressional Record* database in Lexis Advance, select "Browse" and "Sources." Use the "Search for a source" search box to search for the *Congressional Record*. Add that source as a search filter.

Execute the search and find the document indicated below for your problem set. (Hints: Be sure to type the search terms exactly as they appear below, including the quotations, and then "Search within results" for the exact date given.)

Congressional Record Search

Problem Set A	Search Phrase: "Homeowners Protection Act of 1998"
	Document: Senate debate ("Additional Statements") on July 17, 1998
Problem Set B	Search Phrase: "Lobbying Disclosure Act of 1995"
	Document: Extended remarks in the House on December 4, 1995
Problem Set C	Search Phrase: "promoting safe and stable families amendments"
	Document: Senate debate (not the "Chamber Action") on December 13, 2001
Problem Set D	Search Phrase: "Assistive Technology Act of 2004"
	Document: House debate on October 8, 2004
Problem Set E	Search Phrase: Indian Tribal Justice Act
	Document: Conference Report on H.R. 1268 on November 19, 1993

Skim the floor debate, and answer the *Congressional Record* questions, below, for your problem set. (Hint: Often the full text of the bill under consideration will be reproduced in the *Congressional Record*. Scroll down past the text of the bill to find the answer to the question.)

Congressional Record Questions

Problem Set A	1. According to Senator D'Amato, who benefitted from unnecessary PMI premiums?	2. Where will the bill be sent next?
Problem Set B	1. According to Representative Pelosi, what two principles does the bill protect?	2. What will happen if the House amends the bill (effectively delaying it)?
Problem Set C	1. According to Senator Rockefeller, different versions of this bill were introduced in the House and Senate. What does the House version provide and authorize?	2. Scroll to the end of this document. What is the action taken on this bill?

Problem Set D	1. Representative Kildee mentioned the inclusion of the American Indian consortium as a funded protection and advocacy system. Why will this provision have a tremendous positive impact on Indian country?	2. What action did the House take just before Representative Kildee spoke?
Problem Set E	1. Find the "Joint Explanatory Statement of the Committee of Conference." Briefly, what were the two principal differences between the House bill and the Senate bill?	2. Scroll to the bottom of this document. What was the final action taken by the House?

A. Answer the first *Congressional Record* question for your problem set.

B. Answer the second *Congressional Record* question for your problem set.

II. Locating Legislative History in Committee Testimony

This section requires you to locate committee testimony using ProQuest Congressional. Locate the home page for ProQuest Congressional on your library's computer network. (Hint: ProQuest Congressional is a subscription service. Therefore, you may need a password or code to access this service from a computer outside the library.)

Click on the "Advanced Search" link under "Congressional Publications" (which may be "Legislative & Executive Branch Publications" in some libraries). Change the pull down to "All fields *including* full text," uncheck the boxes and check only "Hearings," and change the date to the exact date ("Date is") for the hearing.

The search phrase and document to be located for each problem set appear below. Enter the entire search phrase in the first search box. Execute the search, and locate the document indicated.

Search Phrase and Document

Problem Set A	Search Phrase: private mortgage insurance
	Document: Hearing on the "Homeowners Protection Act of 1997, S. 318" Senate Committee on Banking, Housing, and Urban Affairs, February 25, 1997

Problem Set B	Search Phrase: lobbying reform
	Document: Hearing on "Reform of Laws Governing Lobbying," House Committee on the Judiciary, May 23, 1995
Problem Set C	Search Phrase: safe and stable families
	Document: Hearing on "Promoting Safe and Stable Families Program," House Committee on Ways and Means, May 10, 2001
Problem Set D	Search Phrase: disabled persons
	Document: Hearing on "Developing Partnerships for Assistive and Universally Designed Technologies for Persons with Disabilities," House Committee on Science, August 4, 1998
Problem Set E	Search Phrase: tribal justice
	Document: Hearing on "Tribal Courts and the Administration of Justice in Indian Country," Senate Committee on Indian Affairs, July 24, 2008

A. Click on the link to this hearing to retrieve a summary describing its contents. Review the summary. Using only the information in the summary, briefly describe the purpose of the hearing.

B. Provide the name of the testifying witness for your problem set, as described below.

Testifying Witness

Problem Set A	President and CEO, Navy Federal Credit Union, who testified on February 25, 1997
Problem Set B	Chair, Professional Ethics and Standards Committee, American League of Lobbyists, who testified on May 23, 1995
Problem Set C	Executive Director, Casey Family Services, who testified on May 10, 2001
Problem Set D	Columnist, Washington Times; representing Blinded American Veterans Foundation
Problem Set E	Judge, Tulalip Tribal Court, Tulalip Tribes of the Tulalip Reservation, Washington; also representing Northwest Tribal Court Judges Association

C. Using the "Links to Retrieve selected transcripts" section following the summary, open the testifying witness's testimony and review the lead. Indicate whether the witness was in support of the legislation and briefly describe the testimony. (Hint: You may need to proceed to the body in some transcripts to answer the questions.)

D. Assume that after reviewing the lead, you decide that you would like to read the testimony of the testifying witness you identified above. Skim the testimony, and answer the testimony question for your problem set, below.

Testimony Question

Problem Set A	How long has the company been automatically canceling PMI for its members when it was no longer needed?
Problem Set B	According to the witness, what does our system of government guarantee?
Problem Set C	According to the witness, why are so many foster children generally considered "hard to place"?
Problem Set D	The witness shares 10 recommendations. What are the first three?
Problem Set E	According to the witness, what did the 2000 Report of Tribal Justice Systems confirm, find, and recommend?

Exercise 7.3
Researching the Legislative History of a Federal Statute with Congress.gov

Name: _____   Due Date: _____

Professor: _____   Section: _____

Goal

To locate documents in the legislative history of a specific federal statute electronically using Congress.gov, the Library of Congress Web site.

Instructions

1. After each question, you will find space to write your answer. This is for your convenience while you are working on the exercise. After you finish your research, you must submit your answers in typewritten form. Do not retype the questions. The answer sheet should contain only the answers to the questions.

2. If you spend more than 15 minutes trying to find the answer to any individual question, use the troubleshooting hints in the General Instructions for this Workbook. If you are still unable to find the answer, stop and seek assistance.

There are no separate problem sets for this exercise.

THE ASSIGNMENT

With electronic research tools, you can research the history of an individual federal statute, or you can search by subject. This exercise requires you to use Congress.gov, a public Web site maintained by the Library of Congress, to research the legislative history of a specific federal statute.

Congress.gov contains a wealth of legislative information. Some of its databases contain historical documents dating back many years, while others contain information only since about 1995. Therefore, you need to assess Congress.gov's coverage to see if it contains the information you need. You can also use Congress.gov to trace the progress of pending bills as they make their way through the legislative process.

Using Congress.gov, you can search in a variety of ways, including by bill number, Public Law number, committee, or subject. You can also conduct word searches in Congress.gov's databases.

Use Congress.gov to research the following matter:

You work for an organization that advocates for greater financial regulation and consumer protection. You know that Congress passed, and the President signed, landmark legislation in 2010 on these very issues, and you wish to research the legislative history of the Act.

Go to Congress.gov and answer the questions below.

I. Click on the "Legislation" link at the top of the page. Enter the following search phrase in the search box and select "All Legislation" on the left:

"wall street reform and consumer protection act" [in quotes]

In the search results, find the "Dodd-Frank Wall Street Reform and Consumer Protection Act." Click on the link for "H.R. 4173" and answer the following questions.

   A. Click on the "Text" tab to see the Enrolled Bill. According to the preamble (right after "An Act" and before the Short Title), what is the purpose of the Act?

   B. Scroll past the Table of Contents. Locate Section 3 of the Act, "Severability." What does this Section say?

II. Go back to the top of the page for H.R. 4173 and click on the "Amendments" tab. On December 10, 2009, Representative Sessions offered an amendment. Locate the amendment, "H.Amdt.518," and open the link.

   A. According to the description, what did this amendment seek to do?

   B. Click on the "Text" tab for H.Amdt.518 to see that Representative Sessions's amendment begins on page H14680 of the *Congressional Record*. To retrieve page "H14680," use your browser's Find feature. Scroll through the text to find Representative Sessions's statement in support of this amendment. According to Representative Sessions, what would this new provision allow trial lawyers to do?

C. Go back to the page for "H.Amdt.518" for Representative Sessions's amendment. Check the status of the amendment under "Actions." Did the amendment pass? What was the vote?

III. Go back to the page for H.R. 4173. Near the top of the page you will find a link to the Latest Conference Report: H. Rep. 111-517. Click on this link, and then click on "PDF" to answer the following questions.

  A. Go to the "Joint Explanatory Statement of the Committee of Conference," beginning on page 865 (after the text of the bill). What did the Senate amendment do?

  B. Scroll to the section on "Title VII—Wall Street Transparency and Accountability." Briefly, what does the conference report establish?

IV. Go back to the page for H.R. 4173. On what date did the President sign the bill as Public Law 111-203? (Hint: Look for Action(s).)

Chapter 8
FEDERAL ADMINISTRATIVE LAW RESEARCH

Exercise 8.1
Researching Federal Administrative Regulations from a Statute

Name: _____   Due Date: _____

Professor: _____   Section: _____

Goals

1. To locate and interpret regulations in the *Code of Federal Regulations* (C.F.R.).
2. To locate and interpret regulatory history in the *Federal Register*.

Instructions

1. After each question, you will find space to write your answer. This is for your convenience while you are working on the exercise. After you finish your research, you must submit your answers in typewritten form. Do not retype the questions. The answer sheet should contain only the answers to the questions.

2. If you spend more than 15 minutes trying to find the answer to any individual question, use the troubleshooting hints in the General Instructions for this Workbook. If you are still unable to find the answer, stop and seek assistance.

3. You can complete this exercise using print resources, Lexis, or Westlaw. Be sure to follow your professor's instruction (if any) regarding resources you are permitted or required to use for this exercise. If you complete this exercise in print, reshelve all books as soon as you finish using them.

There are no separate problem sets for this exercise.

128 Basic Legal Research Workbook

THE ASSIGNMENT

A client has come to you with a client matter, set out below. The client matter is an issue addressed by a federal statute and implementing regulations published in the *Code of Federal Regulations* (C.F.R.) and the *Federal Register*. You have decided that you need to research the implementing regulations to understand completely how the statute applies to your client's situation. This exercise will guide you through the process of researching federal regulations.

You can complete the exercise using print resources, WestlawNext, or Lexis Advance.

I. Review Questions

A. How often, and on what schedule, is the C.F.R. published?

B. One way to locate regulations in the C.F.R. is through cross-references to the C.F.R. in U.S.C.A. and U.S.C.S. Briefly describe a second way to locate regulations in the C.F.R.

C. Are regulations in the C.F.R. mandatory or persuasive authority on an issue within an agency's jurisdiction? Be sure to explain your answer.

II. Researching Federal Regulations Using Statutory Annotations

One way to locate federal regulations is through the annotations following the enabling statute in U.S.C.S. and U.S.C.A. Your client has come to you with the following matter, which requires regulatory research:

> Your client, Second Amendment Industries, would like to import and sell toy or look-alike guns. Some of the guns will be realistic looking and intended for use in television and film productions. Some of the guns will be small replicas intended for decoration. The federal government requires toy and look-alike guns to contain markings indicating that they are not real firearms. You need to find out if the federal requirements apply to the products your client wants to import.

A. The federal statute that applies to your client's products is 15 U.S.C. § 5001, Penalties for entering into commerce of imitation firearms. Locate this section of the federal code in U.S.C.A. (in print or in WestlawNext) or U.S.C.S. (in print or in Lexis Advance), and answer the questions below.

1. Review the acts prohibited under the statute. Would it be unlawful for your client to import toy or look-alike guns that do not contain the required markings? Be sure to explain your answer.

2. Review the portion of the statute that describes the required markings. The statute defines the required markings but then grants authority to the Secretary of Commerce to alter those requirements. What authority does the Secretary of Commerce have with respect to look-alike guns used in television and films?

3. The Secretary of Commerce has adopted regulations published in the C.F.R. implementing the requirements of the statute. Review the statutory annotations and find the cross-reference to the regulations. Provide the citation to the portion of the C.F.R. that contains the regulations. The relevant portion may be identified by Title and section number followed by the notation "et seq.", or it may be identified by Title and Part. Both types of references indicate that relevant regulations appear in multiple sections of the C.F.R. (Hints: In WestlawNext, look under the "Context and Analysis" tab to locate cross-references to the *Code of Federal Regulations*. In Lexis Advance, scroll to the bottom of the page, to "Research References & Practice Aids," to locate cross-references to the *Code of Federal Regulations*.)

4. Look up the section or Part you identified for Question A3, above, in the C.F.R. in print or by clicking on the appropriate link. (Hint: If the relevant portion was identified by Part, locate the first section in the Part.) Read the regulation. The marking requirements do not apply to decorative objects that meet certain size requirements. What are those size requirements?

5. The C.F.R. includes references to the *Federal Register* (FR) volume and page where the regulation was published before it was codified in the C.F.R. In print, the reference may appear in brackets immediately following the regulation or at the beginning of the Part, directly after the table of contents. In WestlawNext and Lexis Advance, *Federal Register* references follow the text of the section.

   a. Locate the citation to the *Federal Register* notice published on January 23, 2013 that refers to the regulation you located. Provide the citation, as it appears in the C.F.R., to the *Federal Register* volume and page number. (Hint: The *Federal Register* is abbreviated "FR" in the C.F.R. and in Lexis and Westlaw. "Fed. Reg." is the abbreviation often used in citations.)

   b. Review that same section of the C.F.R. and find the citation to an earlier version of the regulation published in the *Federal Register* on October 26, 1992. Give the citation to the *Federal Register* as it appears in the C.F.R.

B. Just as statutory research often requires you to research a statutory scheme, federal administrative law research often requires you to research a regulatory scheme. To do this, you will need to review the table of contents for the C.F.R. Part containing regulations relevant to your client matter.

   In WestlawNext or Lexis Advance: From the regulation you read for Question A4, above, click on the "Table of Contents" (TOC) link to view the table of contents. (Hint: You may need to scroll up or down to view the entire table of contents for the Part.)

   In Print: From the regulation you read for Question A4, above, turn back to the beginning of the C.F.R. Part to locate the table of contents for the Part.

   In Online U.S. Government Sources: From the regulation you read for Question A4, above, go to the Government Printing Office's Federal Digital System site (www.gpo.gov/fdsys) and use the "Retrieve by Citation" link to enter the citation and find the table of contents.

   1. Using the table of contents, locate the C.F.R. section that addresses waivers from the marking requirements. Provide the title and section number.

2. Review the C.F.R. section. What must your client do to apply for a waiver from the marking requirements for the look-alike guns it wants to import for use in television and film productions?

III. Researching Regulatory History in the *Federal Register*

Having researched your client's question using the C.F.R., you decide that you would like to learn more about the regulatory history of an applicable C.F.R. section. The *Federal Register* prints regulations, proposed regulations, and a brief description of the regulatory history of codified regulations.

The *Federal Register* entry for your regulation begins with the name of the implementing agency. Many, though not all, *Federal Register* entries also contain sections titled "Summary," "Effective Date," "Further Information," and "Supplemental Information" with information on the regulatory history of the section. The final regulations, as they appear in the C.F.R., appear only after these sections.

The regulation you located in Part IIA, above, exempted decorative objects below a particular size from the marking requirements. To find out more about the size limitation in the regulation, locate the *Federal Register* entry you located in Question IIA5(b), above, from October 26, 1992.

In WestlawNext or Lexis Advance: Click on the link to the *Federal Register* (FR) citation following the text of the regulation or enter the citation to retrieve the document. Depending on which service you use, this may take you to the beginning of the entry, or it may link directly to the first reference to the regulation within the entry. You may need to scroll up or down in the document to find the portions describing the changes to the regulation to answer the question below. (Hint: Be sure to use the link or citation to the *Federal Register* for October 26, 1992 that appears after the section you located for Part IIA, above, concerning the size requirements; links following other sections may not retrieve the correct information.)

In Print: Locate the *Federal Register* set in your library. To locate the issue you need, use the *Federal Register* Date chart. The citation refers directly to the page where the amended regulation appears. You will need to review earlier portions of the entry describing the changes to the regulation to answer the question below.

In Online U.S. Government Sources: From the regulation you found for Question A5(b), above, go to the Government Printing Office's Federal Digital System site (www.gpo.gov/fdsys) and use the "Retrieve by Citation" link to enter the citation to the Federal Register.

Review the "Description and Explanation of Proposed Changes" to the rule. (Hint: You may have to scroll up or down to find it.) Why did the Under Secretary of Commerce adopt a size limitation for exempting decorative objects, and why did the Secretary choose the particular dimension set out in the rule?

Exercise 8.2
Researching Federal Administrative Regulations Using Government Web Sites

Name: _____   Due Date: _____

Professor: _____   Section: _____

Goal

To locate federal administrative materials in the *Code of Federal Regulations* (C.F.R.) and *Federal Register* using the online Federal Digital System and federal agency Web sites.

Instructions

1. After each question, you will find space to write your answer. This is for your convenience while you are working on the exercise. After you finish your research, you must submit your answers in typewritten form. Do not retype the questions. The answer sheet should contain only the answers to the questions.

2. If you spend more than 15 minutes trying to find the answer to any individual question, use the troubleshooting hints in the General Instructions for this Workbook. If you are still unable to find the answer, stop and seek assistance.

There are no separate problem sets for this exercise.

THE ASSIGNMENT

This exercise requires you to use government Web sites to locate federal administrative materials. For this exercise, you will use electronic sources to research legal issues raised by your client, Newton Laboratories.

I. Researching Federal Regulations Using an Agency Web Site

The federal government makes much administrative material available free of charge via the Internet. Like federal legislative history, federal administrative law research is easily accomplished using government Web sites. Some government Web sites, such as the Government Printing Office's Federal Digital System (www.gpo.gov/fdsys), contain the full text of the C.F.R. Others, such as agency Web sites, limit their coverage to laws, regulations, and other materials in the subject area the agency regulates. If you practice regularly in an area of law regulated by a federal agency, you will become familiar with the agency sites and the unique types of information they contain. A list of agency websites is at www.usa.gov.

134   Basic Legal Research Workbook

Use the federal government Web sites listed below to research the following question raised by your client:

Your client, Newton Laboratories, is a chemical manufacturer. It is subject to the Occupational Safety and Health (OSH) Act and must comply with Occupational Safety and Health Administration (OSHA) standards and regulations. Newton Laboratories received a citation from an OSHA inspector for several violations of the OSH Act. Newton Laboratories is not sure it can abate (i.e., correct) the safety violations within the time prescribed by the citation. You need to research OSHA penalties to find out your client's potential liability for failing to abate the safety violations within the time prescribed in the citation.

A. First you need to find the provisions of the OSH Act of 1970. You know that OSHA provides access to occupational safety laws and regulations, so you decide to begin with the agency's Web site. Go to www.osha.gov to locate the information you need.

There are several ways to locate the act. Click "Regulations" on the OSHA homepage, then select "OSHA Law and Regulations." You can also locate the act by using the search box to search for the OSH Act or by searching through the A-Z Index.

1. Click on the link for the OSH Act (or "Complete OSH Act"). Review the table of contents for the OSH Act and locate the section regarding penalties. Provide the section number.

2. Click on the link to the section. The section sets out penalties for violations of the OSH Act. If an employer receives a citation for a violation and fails to correct the violation within the time prescribed, what is the maximum penalty the employer faces?

3. A reference to the Public Law that amended this section appears to the right of the statutory text. Provide the Public Law number and briefly explain how the Public Law amended this section. (Hint: Use the explanation provided with the Public Law number; do not research the Historical Notes.)

B. Because the statute sets only a maximum penalty, you must research regulations regarding penalties to determine who sets the actual amount of any penalty. You can locate regulations on the OSHA Web site in several ways. You may use the "Regulations" tab. You can also look up Regulations or

Standards in the A-Z Index. (Hint: When you locate the page with Regulations or Standards, be sure to choose the option to view "All.")

Locate the link to Title 29 of the C.F.R., Part 1903, addressing Inspections, Citations, and Proposed Penalties. Click on the link to bring up an outline of C.F.R. sections within Part 1903. Locate the regulation that addresses failure to correct a violation for which a citation has been issued.

1. Provide the number of the section (also called a "Standard") you located.

2. Review the section. Who notifies the employer of a failure to correct a violation and of the additional penalty proposed?

II. Researching Federal Regulations Using General Government Research Web Sites

A. Although an agency Web site is a convenient source for administrative information, it is not an official source for the regulations. The Federal Digital System, operated by the Government Printing Office (GPO), is the official electronic source for federal regulations. To continue your research in an official database, access the Federal Digital System at:

www.gpo.gov/fdsys

Because Newton Laboratories may not be able to abate the safety violations by the date specified in the citation, you need to find out how to request an extension of time from the agency. Using the search functions on the Federal Digital System Web site, look up 29 C.F.R. § 1903.14a, concerning petitions for modification of an abatement date. (Hint: You should be able to retrieve the regulation from its citation. If you do not find the regulation in the most current year's C.F.R., use the prior year's C.F.R.)

1. What is the title of this section?

2. Review the regulation. What is the deadline for filing a petition to modify the abatement date?

B. The official source for all federal regulations is the C.F.R.; the Federal Digital System provides electronic access to these official regulations. Unlike commercial sources such as Lexis and Westlaw, the official print and electronic versions of the C.F.R. are not continuously updated to include changes published in the *Federal Register*. However, the Federal Digital System site does provide online access to C.F.R. Parts Affected as recently as the past 24 hours (under the link for the List of CFR Sections Affected).

The government also has a version of the C.F.R. that is continuously updated: the e-CFR. The e-CFR is a version of the C.F.R. that is updated daily to incorporate changes to regulations published in the *Federal Register*. You can use the e-CFR to update research from an official version of the C.F.R. You can access the e-CFR through the *Code of Federal Regulations* page in the Federal Digital System.

1. Read the "User Notice" at the beginning of the e-CFR. Although the e-CFR is updated daily, it is not a source you should cite for a regulation. Why?

2. The safety regulation Newton Laboratories was cited for violating concerned employee exposure to chromium. Browse the e-CFR to locate 29 C.F.R. § 1910.1026, the regulation governing chromium exposure. Scroll to the end of the regulation. Provide the date and *Federal Register* citation of the most recent amendment to this regulation.

3. Now go back to the Federal Digital System homepage (www.gpo.gov/fdsys). Browse the Federal Register (in the menu bar on the right side of the screen) to retrieve the *Federal Register* page containing the change to 29 C.F.R. § 1910.1026 that you found in Question 2, above. (Hint: Look for the link to the Occupational Safety and Health Administration.) Which paragraph of this regulation was amended? (Hints: You can use the year and page number to search the *Federal Register* by citation. Click the link on the left side of the screen. Be sure to identify the change to 29 C.F.R. § 1910.1026 and not any other section.)

Exercise 8.3
Researching Federal Administrative Regulations on Your Own

Name: _____   Due Date: _____

Professor: _____   Section: _____

Goal

To locate and interpret regulations in the *Code of Federal Regulations* (C.F.R.).

Instructions

1. After each question, you will find space to write your answer. This is for your convenience while you are working on the exercise. After you finish your research, you must submit your answers in typewritten form. Do not retype the questions. The answer sheet should contain only the answers to the questions.

2. If you spend more than 30 minutes researching the client matter for your problem set, use the troubleshooting hints in the General Instructions for this Workbook. If you are still unable to find the answer, stop and seek assistance.

3. If you conduct research in print, reshelve all books as soon as you finish using them.

There are no separate problem sets for this exercise.

THE ASSIGNMENT

Your client has approached you with the client matter below. The client matter is an issue that can be answered by reference to federal regulations. You need to research federal regulations relevant to the client matter.

You can complete the exercise using print resources, government Web sites, WestlawNext, or Lexis Advance.

Client Matter

Your client manufactures children's safety helmets used for skateboarding and rollerblading. The client has prepared new marketing materials that include a photo of a group of children on skateboards, rollerblades, and bicycles wearing the client's helmets. Nothing in the marketing materials expressly states that the helmets are bicycle helmets, but nothing indicates that skateboarding and rollerblading are the only activities for which the helmet provides protection. You are concerned about the impression the marketing campaign may create. You need to find out whether including a photo of bicyclists wearing the helmet in the marketing materials subjects your client to Consumer Product Safety Commission regulations governing bicycle helmets, and if so, how the required warnings on the helmet label must appear.

I. Locating Federal Regulations

A. Locate regulations that resolve the client matter, and provide the title and section numbers for the regulations.

B. Explain how you located the regulations.

II. Resolving the Client Matter

Based on the results of your research, explain whether the regulations likely apply to your client's product and how the word "Warning" has to appear on a bicycle helmet label.

Chapter 9
ELECTRONIC SEARCH TECHNIQUES

Exercise 9.1
Electronic Search Techniques

Name: _____   Due Date: _____

Professor: _____   Section: _____

Goals

1. To understand how differences in database coverage affect search results.
2. To understand how to limit and refine search results.
3. To understand how to use Boolean search techniques in WestlawNext and Lexis Advance.

Instructions

1. After each question, you will find space to write your answer. This is for your convenience while you are working on the exercise. After you finish your research, you must submit your answers in typewritten form. Do not retype the questions. The answer sheet should contain only the answers to the questions.

2. If you spend more than five minutes trying to find the answer to any individual question, use the troubleshooting hints in the General Instructions for this Workbook. If you are still unable to find the answer, stop and seek assistance.

There are no separate problem sets for this exercise.

THE ASSIGNMENT

The purpose of this exercise is to illustrate how electronic search results differ depending on the scope of the database you select and the Boolean (terms and connectors) search options you use.

To illustrate the effects of the search options, some of the searches in this exercise will retrieve very large numbers of documents, while others will retrieve very few. Remember, however, that a search is neither effective nor ineffective based solely on the number of documents it retrieves. If many authorities are relevant to your research, you want to retrieve all the relevant documents. If few authorities are relevant, you want to be able to target those few authorities. The purpose of this exercise is simply to show you how various search options will affect your search results. In each research project you do, you will have to decide which approaches are most likely to retrieve the information you need.

The first step in electronic searching is selecting an electronic service in which to search. For this exercise, you will use WestlawNext and Lexis Advance. The questions that follow direct you to execute a variety of searches.

I. WestlawNext

A. Selecting a Database or Jurisdiction

If you decide to research in WestlawNext, you may select a database in which to execute a search. The database you select defines the content through which WestlawNext will look for your search terms. The scope of your research project will determine the appropriate database(s) in which to search.

In WestlawNext you can designate a database (including a jurisdiction) for your search by selecting from the "Browse" box. You can also designate a jurisdiction in the jurisdiction box next to the universal search box. Finally, you can designate a jurisdiction *after* you execute your search by using the "Narrow" filters on the left side of the search results screen.

For the questions below, assume that you need to research state case law concerning crimes associated with illegal drug use among students at school.

1. Select the jurisdiction for "All States." (Hint: Be sure to de-select any federal jurisdiction.) Execute this search:

    student and school and drug and illegal

    How many cases does the search retrieve?

2. Now change the jurisdiction to "California," and execute the same search. How many documents does this search retrieve?

If you were researching the law of all 50 states, "All States" might be an appropriate jurisdiction for your search. If you were researching only California state law, however, "California" would be a better choice, because it would limit the search results to authority from California state courts.

3. Assume that you decided to change the scope of your search to include cases from the California state courts and federal cases from the Ninth Circuit. From the jurisdiction menu, select "California" and "9th Circuit." Execute the same search as above. How many cases does the search retrieve? (Note that this search will also automatically retrieve relevant U.S. Supreme Court cases and federal district court cases within the Ninth Circuit.)

4. Now assume that you want to search only California state cases, Ninth Circuit cases, and federal district court cases from California. Click the View for Cases on the left side of the search results screen. Use the "Narrow" filters to designate your jurisdictions to include all California state cases, all Ninth Circuit cases, and all cases from the federal district courts in California. (Hint: Be sure to select all the federal district courts in California.) How many cases does the search retrieve?

B. Constructing and Executing a Search—Boolean Search Techniques

After you select a database, the next steps are constructing and executing a search. WestlawNext allows you to search with or without Boolean search commands. Effective use of Boolean search commands can improve your search results. The following questions illustrate the use of connectors and search phrases.

1. Connectors

The connectors you use to connect search terms can greatly affect the search results.

For questions a and b, below, assume that you need to continue your research into crimes associated with illegal drug use among students at school. Now, however, you are researching all federal law.

a. From the jurisdiction menu, select "All Federal." Type this phrase into the search box, and execute the search:

> student and school and drug and illegal

How many cases does the search retrieve?

b. Now change the connectors from "and" to "/p" (meaning "within the same paragraph"). (Hint: You can also use the "Advanced Search" option and type this phrase into the box designated for "All of these terms.") Execute this search:

> student /p school /p drug /p illegal

How many cases does the revised search retrieve?

The more restrictive the connectors, the fewer documents the search retrieves. The broader the connectors, the more documents the search retrieves. "And" is the broadest connector.

2. **Search phrases**

Another way to alter your search results is to group terms together in search phrases.

The notion of a bona fide residence may arise in cases involving qualifications for municipal employment, voting, taxing, licensing, and other areas. Assume that you are researching bona fide residences in Illinois and want to research Illinois cases.

a. Designate "Illinois" as your jurisdiction. Type this phrase into the search box and execute the search:

> bona fide residence

How many cases does the search retrieve?

b. Go to the "Advanced Search" page. Type that same phrase into the box designated for "This exact phrase," and execute the search. How many documents does the revised search retrieve?

To search for a particular phrase in WestlawNext, use the Advanced Search box designated for "This exact phrase." Do not use the boxes designated for "Any of these terms" or "All of these terms" because the results will include irrelevant cases.

C. Limiting and Refining Search Results

You can limit and refine your search by using the "Document Fields" in the Advanced search option or the "Narrow" filters on the left side of the case results screen.

1. A "document field" is an individual component of a document, such as its citation or title. When you use a field restriction, the search is run only within the specified component of the document.

    Assume you need to research federal court cases within the Seventh Circuit in which the State of Illinois is a party. Designate "7th Circuit" in the jurisdiction box next to the search box. Click on "advanced" to gain access to the advanced search options. Type "Illinois" into the "Name/Title" box under "Document Fields." Execute the search. How many cases does the search retrieve?

Note that this search retrieves every case in which the term "Illinois" appears in the case name. Although this will retrieve decisions in which the State of Illinois is a party, it retrieves many other decisions, too.

2. Now refine your search to find cases involving quid pro quo (literally "this for that") in employment discrimination. Click on "advanced" to gain access to the advanced search options. Type "quid pro quo" into the box designated for "This exact phrase." (Hint: Be sure that "Illinois" still appears in the "Name/Title" box.) Execute the search. How many cases does the revised search retrieve?

3. Refine your search further by using the "Narrow" filters on the left side of the search results screen. (Hint: Be sure to designate "Cases" as your "View.") Select the Seventh Circuit as your Jurisdiction, and select the topic "Employment & Labor." Apply the filters, and execute the search. How many cases does your revised search retrieve?

4. Click on the "View" for "Secondary Sources." Provide the title of an article from 2007 involving the case *Estes v. Ill. Dep't of Human Servs.*

Note that you may narrow your case search using other filtering criteria, including date, reported status, judge, attorney, law firm, Key Number, party, and docket number. These options appear under "Narrow" on the left side of the search results screen.

II. Lexis Advance

A. Selecting a Database or Jurisdiction

Just as you can select a database or jurisdiction for your search in WestlawNext, you can select a database or jurisdiction for your search in Lexis Advance. You can select a database or jurisdiction using the drop-down menu in the "Filters" button in the red search box. You can also select a database or jurisdiction using the browse options above the red search box. Finally, you can select a database or jurisdiction *after* you execute your search by using the "Narrow By" options on the left side of the search results screen or the sub-tabs along the top of the search results screen.

Assume that you are researching adverse possession.

1. Using the jurisdiction drop-down filter in the red search box, limit your initial search to the United States Supreme Court. Enter the following search in the red search box:

    adverse possession

    Execute the search, and click on the "Cases" sub-tab. How many cases does this search retrieve?

2. Now change the jurisdiction filter to "Virginia" and execute the new search. How many cases does this new search retrieve?

3. Assume that you wish to research only Virginia Supreme Court cases. Using the "Narrow By" options on the left side of the search results screen, find the "Court" options. Click on the link for the Virginia Supreme Court. How many cases does this new search retrieve?

4. Assume that you decide to expand the scope of your search to include federal cases. In the "Filters" menu in the search box, designate "Include related Federal content." Execute the new search. How many cases does this new search retrieve?

5. To find related secondary sources, click the sub-tab "Secondary Materials." Provide the title of a 2012 law review article from the Virginia Journal of Social Policy and the Law.

B. Constructing and Executing a Search—Boolean Search Techniques

Like WestlawNext, Lexis Advance allows you to search with or without Boolean search commands.

1. Connectors

Just as you can use connectors in WestlawNext to refine your search, you can use connectors in Lexis Advance to refine your search.

a. Clear the search box. (Hint: Be sure that your jurisdiction is set to "Virginia" and "related Federal content.") Type this phrase into the search box, and execute the search:

> adverse /s possession

How many cases does the search retrieve?

b. Now replace the "/s" with "/2" so that the new search phrase reads as follows:

> adverse /2 possession

How many cases does this search retrieve?

The connector "/s" tells Lexis Advance to search for any document in which the word "adverse" appears in the same sentence as the word "possession." As a result, your search results may include documents that have nothing to do with adverse possession (because the words are used in an entirely different context, even if in the same sentence). In contrast, the connector "/2" tells Lexis Advance to search for any document in which the word "adverse" appears within two words of the word "possession." These results are more likely to include documents that use the phrase "adverse possession."

Lexis Advance allows you to use other connectors to refine your search. These are available in the "Filters" drop-down from the search box by selecting "Advanced Search."

2. **Search Phrases**

In Lexis Advance you can also refine your search using Boolean commands by using the "Filters" drop-down menu from the search box and selecting "Advanced Search."

a. Clear the red search box, and open the Filter and click on Advanced Search. (Hint: Be sure your jurisdiction is set to "Virginia" and "Include related Federal content.") Type this phrase in the "Search Terms" box, designate "include this exact word or phrase," and click "Add to Search." (Note that the phrase appears in quotation marks in the red search box.)

> adverse possession

Execute the search. How many cases does the search retrieve?

b. Now assume that you wish to eliminate results that involve adverse possession of housing. Click on the "Filters" button, click on "Advanced Search," and designate "Exclude these words" in the "Search Terms." Add the search phrase "hous!" and click "Add to Search." Your search phrase in the red search box should read as follows:

"adverse possession" and not hous!

Execute the search. How many cases does the search retrieve?

The extender "!" tells Lexis Advance to search for any word that starts with "hous," including "house," "houses," and "housing." Lexis Advance has other extenders, which are listed under "Connectors" in the "Advanced Search" tab. Note that this search may eliminate more results than you wish, because a document may use the words "house," "houses," or "housing" even if the document does not involve adverse possession of housing.

C. Limiting and Refining Search Results

You can limit and refine your search results in Lexis Advance using the content category, jurisdiction, and practice-area menus in the red search box. You can also use the "Narrow By" options on the left side of the search results screen.

1. Using the same search phrase and jurisdictions from B.2.b, above, in the red search box click on "Filters," and select "Category." Limit your content results to "Briefs, Pleadings and Motions." Execute the search. Provide the name of a case in which a party filed a brief using the phrase "adverse possession," but not the words "house," "houses," or "housing," in the United States Supreme Court in 2007.

2. Now unclick "Briefs, Pleadings, and Motions" so that the filter is set for "Virginia" and "related Federal content." Using the same search phrase from C.1, above, execute the search. Using the "Narrow By" options on the left side of the search results screen, click on "Timeline." Designate dates from January 1, 2000 to January 2, 2010 and click "OK." How many cases does this search retrieve?

Chapter 10
RESEARCH PLANNING

Exercise 10.1
Developing and Executing a Research Plan

Name: _____   Due Date: _____

Professor: _____   Section: _____

Goal

To develop and execute a comprehensive research plan to locate authority on a legal issue.

Instructions

1. After each question, you will find space to write your answer. This is for your convenience while you are working on the exercise. After you finish your research, you must submit your answers in typewritten form. Do not retype the questions. The answer sheet should contain only the answers to the questions.

2. Reshelve all books as soon as you finish using them.

Problem Set
(circle one)   A   B   C   D   E

THE ASSIGNMENT

Your client has come to you for advice about the legal questions set out in your problem set. To answer the legal questions, you will need to research the law using a variety of research tools. To complete this exercise, you will need to develop and execute a research plan. The questions in this exercise will guide you through the research planning process and help you locate authorities relevant to the legal questions. If appropriate for your problem set, your professor will assign a jurisdiction for your research.

Legal Questions

Problem Set A: State Common Law Research
Real Estate Agent v. Data Retention Company

Your client, a self-employed real estate agent, contracted with a data retention company to store computer data on the retention company's computer servers. The data retention company's servers failed, and your client's data was lost. It cannot be recovered. The lost data consists primarily of customer lists. Your client would like to recover damages from the data retention company. Your client may have valid claims for conversion or violation of a bailment agreement.

You need to find the answers to the following questions: (1) What are the elements of conversion and bailment claims under state law? (2) Assuming that the customer lists qualify as personal property under state law, does your client likely have a valid claim under either theory?

(Hint: In answering the second question, assume that the customer lists qualify as personal property.)

Problem Set B: State Statutory Research
Employee v. Advertising Firm

Your client has contacted you about a potential discrimination claim against his employer, an advertising firm. About a year ago, he underwent genetic testing as part of a company-sponsored "wellness program." The lab that conducted the tests sent all employees' test results to the employer, which then forwarded the results to individual employees. The genetic test showed that your client is genetically predisposed to Alzheimer's disease, although he does not presently show any signs of the disease. Shortly after receiving the test results, your client was taken off two high profile projects at work, and he has been reassigned to a less prestigious work group. Your client suspects that his employer reviewed the genetic test results and made the work changes based on the results of the test.

You need to find the answers to the following questions: (1) Does state law prohibit employment discrimination based on genetic information or the results of a genetic test? (2) Do the employer's actions, if based on the test results, constitute employment discrimination?

Problem Set C: Federal Statutory Research
Discharged Employee v. Appliance Repair Company

Your client is an appliance repair company. The company recently fired an employee who is now threatening to file suit against the company. The discharged employee and a supervisor in another department at the company had been in conflict with each other because the discharged employee's ex-husband is dating the supervisor. The individuals' personal animosity was well-known within the office and created a stressful work environment. A month ago, the supervisor's car was vandalized in the company's parking lot. The company suspects that the employee caused the damage. The company conducted an internal investigation and asked the employee to submit to a polygraph examination. The employee refused. The company then fired the employee, both for refusing the test and for creating a difficult work environment for other employees. You know that federal law restricts the circumstances under which an employer can require an employee to take a lie detector test.

You need to find the answers to the following questions: (1) Was the company permitted to require a polygraph examination as part of its ongoing investigation into the vandalism incident? (2) To make out a prima facie case of a violation of federal law restricting employer use of polygraph tests, must the discharged employee show that her refusal to take the test was the sole reason for her termination?

Problem Set D: State Procedural Research
Real Estate Agent v. Data Retention Company

You represent the self-employed real estate agent in the action against the data retention company as described in Problem Set A. You filed suit in state court on behalf of your client. The data retention company has filed a motion to dismiss the claims, arguing that customer lists do not qualify as personal property for purposes of the claims asserted. You missed two weeks of work because of illness and are concerned you may not be able to complete your response to the motion in time. You would like to file a motion for an extension of time to respond to the motion.

Locate the state procedural rule governing extension or enlargement of time and answer the following questions: (1) Under what circumstances can the court grant your request if you make it before the deadline for the response? (2) What must you show to obtain an extension or enlargement of time if you make the request after the deadline for the response?

(Hint: Use only the language of the rule, not cases interpreting the rule, to answer these questions.)

> **Problem Set E: Federal Procedural Research**
> *Discharged Employee v. Appliance Repair Company*
>
> You represent the appliance repair company in the action brought by a discharged employee as described in Problem Set C, above. The discharged employee filed suit in federal court against your client. The case proceeded to trial, and the jury rendered a verdict in favor of the discharged employee. You filed a motion for a new trial. Before the presiding judge could decide the motion, she died. The case was assigned to a successor judge, who must now resolve the motion for a new trial.
>
> Locate the federal rule of civil procedure that applies when a judge is unable to proceed with a case, and research cases applying the rule to answer the following questions: (1) What must a successor judge certify to complete the case? (2) Can a successor judge who did not preside over the original trial decide a motion for a new trial?
>
> (Hint: You will need to research cases interpreting the rule to answer the second question.)

I. Obtaining Preliminary Information

List the preliminary information you know about the problem: due date, work product expected, limits on research tools to be used, jurisdiction, and whether persuasive authority should be located.

II. Drafting a Preliminary Issue Statement

Prepare a preliminary issue statement.

III. Generating Search Terms

List your search terms. Be sure to expand the breadth and depth of the list. (Hint: The charts in Exercise 2.1 can help you with this process.)

IV. Planning and Executing Your Research Plan

A. Search for primary mandatory authority first. List the sources you plan to consult in the order you plan to consult them. For each source, indicate whether you will conduct your research in print or with electronic services and why you chose print or electronic media. (Hint: Remember that even in a search for primary mandatory authority, secondary sources can often be a good starting point because they provide background information and citations to primary authority.)

B. Begin your research, keeping notes as you work. Indicate below the order in which you actually consulted each source. If the order differed from your original plan, explain why. In addition, list any electronic searches you executed.

C. List up to three primary mandatory authorities you plan to use to analyze the legal questions you are researching. Briefly explain how you located each authority and why you plan to use it.

D. Remember to update each authority you plan to use. List the steps you took to update each authority.

E. Assess your research results. Do you need to locate persuasive authority (primary persuasive authority or secondary authority) to complete your analysis? Why or why not?

F. If you do not need to locate persuasive authority, skip to Question J, below.

If you do need to locate persuasive authority, plan your research for locating this additional authority. List the sources you plan to consult in the order you plan to consult them. For each source, indicate whether you will conduct your research in print or with electronic services and why you chose print or electronic media. (Hint: Remember that secondary sources can be effective for locating primary persuasive authority.)

G. After planning your research path for locating persuasive authority, continue your research, keeping notes as you work. Indicate below the order in which you actually consulted each source. If the order differed from your original plan, explain why. In addition, list any electronic searches you executed.

H. List up to three persuasive authorities (primary or secondary) you plan to use to analyze the legal questions you are researching. Briefly explain how you located each authority and why you plan to use it.

I. Remember to update each persuasive authority you plan to use. List the steps you took to update each authority.

J. Assess your research results. Has your research come full circle, in that the authorities you have located have begun to refer back to each other and the new authorities you locate fail to reveal significant new information?

K. If the answer to Question J, above, is yes, skip to Part V, below, because your research is complete. If your answer to Question J is no, explain the further steps you plan to take to complete your research.

V. Answering the Legal Questions

Once you have completed your research, you are ready to draft answers to your client's legal questions. Write a brief analysis (1-4 paragraphs) answering the legal questions. Be sure to state the common law, statutory, or procedural rule(s) applicable to the questions and apply the facts of your problem set to the rule(s). If the problem set does not contain sufficient facts for you to analyze the legal questions completely, identify the additional facts you would need to provide a complete answer.